POSSESS THE LAND

Valarie Owen

**All Scripture quotations
from the King James Version
of the Bible unless otherwise stated**

ISBN 0-914307-17-7
**Printed in the United States of America
Copyright © 1983 WORD OF FAITH PUBLISHING
PO Box 819000, Dallas, Texas 75381
All Rights Reserved**

"And gave them the lands of the heathen: and they inherited the labour of the people; That they might observe his statutes, and keep his laws. Praise ye the Lord" (Psalm 105:44,45)

TABLE OF CONTENTS

INTRODUCTION

CHAPTER ONE	ENTERING THE LAND	1
CHAPTER TWO	CONQUERING THE LAND	29
CHAPTER THREE	POSSESSING THE LAND	39
CHAPTER FOUR	JUDGES	57
CHAPTER FIVE	RUTH	73
CHAPTER SIX	THE REIGN OF SAMUEL	79
CHAPTER SEVEN	THE REIGN OF SAUL	91
CHAPTER EIGHT	DAVID AND GOLIATH	101
CHAPTER NINE	THE REIGN OF DAVID	119
CHAPTER TEN	THE REIGN OF SOLOMON	133
CHAPTER ELEVEN	KINGDOM DIVIDED	147
CHAPTER TWELVE	ELIJAH THE TISHBITE	151
CHAPTER THIRTEEN	CHARIOT OF FIRE	161
CHAPTER FOURTEEN	THE MINISTRY OF ELISHA	173
CHAPTER FIFTEEN	RETURN TO JERUSALEM	181

INTRODUCTION

The first five books of the Bible, Genesis through Deuteronomy, are known as the books of the "Law," while the next 12, Joshua through Esther, are referred to as "historical."

The first chapter of Joshua is quoted probably more often by teachers than any other book in the Old Testament. It is believed that this book correctly bears the name of its leading character who was from the tribe of Ephraim. Joshua means "Jehovah is Salvation." The theme of this book is the conquering of Canaan. Before the death of Moses, God commissioned Joshua as leader to carry His people into the land He had promised to them centuries ago. Moses died in the land of Moab, as God had directed, and He buried him in a valley in the land of Moab, in the valley opposite Beth Peor, but to this day no one knows the location of his grave.

Before his death, Moses laid his hands upon Joshua, and God filled him with the spirit of wisdom for the enormous task ahead of him. This book is a partial record of the military campaigns waged by Joshua in his conquest of Canaan, and it ends with the division of the land among the twelve tribes of Israel.

While Joshua speaks to us of man possessing, the book of Judges shows us man in rebellion to God. *"In those days there was no king in Israel: every man did that which was right in his own eyes" (Judges 21:25).* The book of Judges reveals to us the utter failure of the children of Israel, and the persistent grace and mercy of their God. The period of the judges over Israel was tagged as the dark ages of Hebrew history.

Then the short book of Ruth comes to us as a soft evening breeze across parched desert sands. It is the story or history of the domestic affairs of one particular family during the times of the judges, and fitly goes before the books of Samuel because at the close it introduces David.

Originally the two books of Samuel, like the two books of Kings, formed an undivided whole. The divisions came solely for the purpose of clarification to the reader. Book one named after Israel's great Seer, Samuel, covered a transitional period between the Judges and the Monarchy. Samuel was a judge and a prophet. Although he was the last judge, he was not the first prophet, and he was not a king. He served Israel in that "in between" period of her history. Up to this time the priest had played a prominent part in the life of God's people, and the prophet a small part; but the priesthood had become a corrupted thing, and it gave way to the authority of the prophetic office. From this point on the king and the prophet became two offices that supplemented each other. However, the king represented the earthly throne and kingdom, while the prophet had the mind of God in all matters concerning the people.

After God rejected Saul as king over Israel, He sent Samuel to anoint a young man named Daivd. Samuel did not want to anoint David for fear of the consequences, but by the command of God, he went to the house of Jesse, and sought out the new king who would rule after the death of Saul. *"I have made a covenant with my chosen, I have sworn unto David my servant, thy seed will I establish for ever and build up thy throne to all generations" (Psalm 89:3,4).* David and his son, Solomon, shared the desire to make Israel a grand and glorious nation. But, unlike David, Solomon's visions of a land of oriental opulence was tempered neither by sensitivity to the thoughts and feelings of the people of Israel, nor by consideration of their religious values which were so cherished by God's people. One writer stated that Solomon was "born in purple," while his father David knew the plight of economic survival in rugged Palestine. David was a man of war, while Solomon gained a reputation for both wisdom and splendor. Solomon used agreements with Phoenicia to Israel's advantage in every way possible. He updated his army though he never fought a major campaign, he maintained a strong fighting force which included fourteen hundred war chariots and twelve thousand horsemen. Archaeological excavations at Megiddo reveal vast installations for stabling horses in several "chariot and horse cities." Also, three full chapters are given to the description of the building and furnishings of the magnificent temple he built with forced labor. It was made of stone made ready before brought forth, so that neither hammer nor axe nor any tool of iron was heard in the house while it was being built. This magnificent temple represented the Presence of Yahweh. Besides the building of the temple, Solomon built his own palace, the house of the forest of Lebanon, the house of Pharaoh's daughter, and the porch of judgment.

After these great accomplishments, while Solomon was at the height of his fame, God appeared to him for the second time to give him a word of warning. *"And the Lord appeared to Solomon the second time, as he had appeared unto him at Gibeon. And the Lord said unto him, I have heard thy prayer and thy supplication, that thou hast made before me; I have hallowed this house, which thou hast built, to put my name there forever; and mine eyes and mine heart shall be there perpetually. And if thou wilt walk before me, as David, thy father, walked, in integrity of heart, and in uprightness, to do according to all that I have commanded thee, and wilt keep my statutes and mine judgments, Then will I establish the throne of thy kingdom upon Israel for ever, as I promised to David thy father, saying, there shall not fail thee a man upon the throne of Israel. But if ye shall at all turn from following me, ye or your children, and will not keep my commandments and my statutes which I have set before you, but go and serve other Gods, and worship them: Then will I cut off Israel..." (I Kings 9:4-7).*

At this time he was visited by the Queen of Sheba who had heard of the wisdom and fame of Solomon, and she came to see for herself if such could be true. *"Howbeit I believed not the words, until I came, and mine eyes had seen it: and, behold, the half was not told me: thy wisdom and prosperity exceedeth the fame which I heard" (I Kings 10:7).*

But King Solomon loved many heathen women which led to downfall and the tragic split of the Kingdom of Israel. For the third time God appeared to him, and this occasion in condemnation. Solomon had turned from God, now God would turn from him.

It was at this point in Israel's history, that the voice of the prophet Elijah became pronounced. The king had failed, so now the king and the prophet would rule together. Elijah was the prophet of judgment and fire, while Elisha was representative of God's continued mercy and grace. The many miracles performed by both Elijah and Elisah were in keeping with Israel's condition at that time. Miracles were needed due to the idolatrous state of the children of Israel. Idolatry had so gripped the nation that the true and living God was no longer known by them. Here and there were individuals who still believed, but the masses were worshipers of idols.

In I and II Chronicles the history of Israel's rise and fall is rehearsed, and it ends with the destruction of the temple, and their Babylonian captivity of seventy years.

God offered the Kingdom to Israel and she rejected Him; Jesus came preaching the Kingdom of God, and again it was rejected. In Matthew 10:6,7, we read, *"But go rather to the lost sheep of the house of Israel. And as you go, preach, saying, The kingdom of heaven is at hand."* The Kingdom was theirs by right of election, history, and heritage. Thus, our Lord directed His ministry to them and offered to them that which had already been promised to them by God. When Israel rejected their heritage and birthright, the kingdom was offered to those who would accept Him. Praise be to Our Lord that we have been accepted in the Beloved due to the unbelief of Israel. Yet Paul cried out, *"I say then, Hath God cast away his people? God forbid. For I also am an Israelite, of the seed of Abraham, of the tribe of Benjamin. God hath not cast away his people which he foreknew. Wot ye not what the scripture saith of Elias? how he maketh intercession to God against Israel saying, Lord, they have killed thy prophets, and digged down thine altars; and I am left alone, and they seek my life. But what saith the answer of God unto him? I have reserved to myself seven thousand men, who have not bowed the knee to the image of Baal" (Romans 11:1-4).*

Author: Joshua
Date: 14th Century B.C.

Chapter 1

ENTERING THE LAND

The book of Joshua resumes the story of the children of Israel headed for the land flowing with milk and honey which had been promised to Abraham and his descendants. Moses had led them out of Egypt under the mighty hand of God to the plains of Moab. From there to Pisgah Peak in Mount Nebo, across from Jericho, the Lord God showed Moses the Promised Land, and the Lord said, *"...This is the land which I sware unto Abraham, unto*

Isaac, and unto Jacob, saying, I will give it unto thy seed: I have caused thee to see it with thine eyes, but thou shalt not go over thither. So Moses the servant of the Lord died there in the land of Moab, according to the word of the Lord. And he buried him in a valley in the land of Moab, over against Beth-peor: but no man knoweth of his sepulchre unto this day" (Deuteronomy 34:4- 6).

Preparation

"Moses my servant is dead; now therefore arise, go over this Jordan, thou, and all this people, unto the land which I do give to them, even to the children of Israel. Every place that the sole of your foot shall tread upon, that have I given unto you, as I said unto Moses. From the wilderness and this Lebanon even unto the great river, the river Euphrates, all the land of the Hittites, and to the great sea toward the going down of the sun, shall be your coast. There shall not any man be able to stand before thee all the days of thy life: as I was with Moses, so I will be with thee: I will not fail thee, nor forsake thee" (Deuteronomy 1:2-5).

Through the years Joshua had served faithfully at the side of Moses. He was born in Egypt; he was introduced shortly after the children Israel started their journey out of Egypt when Moses instructed him to fight Amalek while he went into the mountain to pray for the victory. Joshua accompanied him to the top of Sinai, when God gave Moses the tables of stone, and returned with him to find the children below worshiping the golden calf fashioned by Aaron, Moses' brother. Joshua ministered in the tabernacle before the establishment of the priesthood. Caleb and Joshua were the only two of the twelve spies who brought back a positive report. They were the only two of that generation who entered the Promised Land. Over and over Joshua had proven faithful in the small things, now God had placed him in charge of His people to take the place of Moses whom God knew face to face.

The name Joshua is equivalent to the name of Jesus, and means "Yahweh is Savior" or salvation of "Yahweh." Just as the first Joshua led in battle and conquered the enemy and possessed the land of Promise, so Jesus Christ has conquered Satan and given us the power to possess our inheritance by using His Name. We cannot study the book of Joshua without realizing it is the book of the inheritance and is linked closely with the Epistle to the Ephesians in the New Testament. In Luke 10:19, we read, *"Behold, I give unto you power to tread on serpents and scorpions and over all the power of the enemy: and nothing shall by any means hurt you."* Jesus told His disciples in John 16:33, that He had already overcome for them: *"These things I have spoken unto you, that in me ye might have peace. In the world ye shall have tribulation: but be of good cheer; I have overcome the world."* This is a most important analysis, and it should open to us the mind of the Sovereign God whom we serve. He told Joshua that the greatest prophet of all time was now dead, but He had chosen another to take his place and lead His children home. God reminded Joshua that He had promised this land to the Israelites centuries before he was born, and it was time to cross over and conquer.

Joshua had the Word of God that He would never fail him, nor would He forsake him. The Blessed Holy Spirit by the pen of Paul wrote these words for our comfort, *"Jesus Christ the same yesterday, and today, and for ever" (Hebrews 13:8).* We have the Word of the Lord that He is the same God today that He was when He led the Israelites into the Promised Land. They had a certain claim upon the Lord, and so do we, if we have received Him as our Lord and Savior. Joshua typifies the Risen One leading us on into the privileges of the new creation. We are blessed with all spiritual blessings "in heavenly places in Christ" (Ephesians 1:3).

Joshua was to take the people across the Jordan, as Moses had led them across the Red Sea some forty years prior. The promise that, *"Every place that the sole of your foot shall tread..."* proved once again that Canaan was a free and sovereign gift of God to Israel. It must be pointed out that neither they nor any of their ancestors had done anything to merit such a heritage. Thus we are all brought to the place where we cry, *"Not by works of righteousness which we have done, but according to His mercy He saved us by the washing of regeneration and renewing of the Holy Spirit, which He shed on us abundantly through Jesus Christ our Saviour" (Titus 3:5,6).* Saints in all generations subscribe to the declaration of Ephesians 2:8,9, *"By grace are ye saved through faith, and that not of yourselves: it is the gift of God; not of works lest any man should boast."* It is not what we can do for God, but what He has done for us. Jesus Christ came not to impose heavy burdens upon us, but to lift them. By His finished work of Calvary, we have inherited the land, but we must recognize that there are enemies in the land with which we must deal. Christians are in a spiritual warfare with the devil. Jesus has won the battle, and we must claim the victory as ours. In I Corinthians 15:57,58, we read, *"But thanks be to God, which giveth us the victory through our Lord Jesus Christ. Therefore, my beloved brethren, be ye stedfast, unmoveable, always abounding in the work of the Lord, forasmuch as ye know that your labour is not in vain in the Lord."*

The children of Israel must cross the Jordan, fight their enemies, drive them out, capture cities, and conquer the Canaanites before they could relax and enjoy their promised inheritance and enter the promised rest of God. They would conquer only as they walked by faith and obedience to the Lord. "It is one thing to have title to an inheritance, but it is quite another thing to make it one's own practically" (Ironsides). Many Christians live their entire life, and go to be with the Lord, and never enter into their full inheritance of peace, and joy, health. All this and more is ours in the Son of God.

Note the extent of Israel's inheritance as outlined by God. It ranged from the Euphrates down to the border of the land of Egypt, and the Mediterranean Sea, and then from the desert of Arabia on the south to Damascus on the north, including all the land of the Hittites; God gave all this to Israel, and for a short time during the reign of Solomon, they possessed most of it. They were to spoil the "ites" in the land, and God promised that no man would be able to oppose them for He would lead the battles. In Obadiah 17, we read, *"But upon mount Zion shall be deliverance, and there shall be holiness; and the house of Jacob shall possess their possessions."* However, we will remember that in Exodus 23:29,30, the Lord told His people that He would not drive out their enemies all at once: *"I will not drive them out from before thee in one year; lest the land become desolate, and the beast of the field multiply against thee. By little and little I will drive them out from before thee, until thou be increased, and inherit the land."* God does not act arbitrarily, but compassionately with respect to His people. There were wild beasts in the land as well as gross idolaters, and Israel was yet too few in number to occupy the entire land. By driving out the Canaanites "little by little" Israel remained totally dependent upon the Lord. God's total purpose in our lives is to lead us gently from self-reliance and teach us to lean completely upon Him for all our needs and desires. No where in the Bible does it indicate that our enemies will be overcome all at once, or once and for all. *"Therefore will the Lord wait that He may be gracious unto you"* (Isaiah 30:18). *"He has many things to say to us, but we are not yet ready for them"* (John 16:12).

Encouragement

"Be strong and of a good courage: for unto this people shalt thou divide for an inheritance the land, which I sware unto their fathers to give them. Only be thou strong and very courageous, that thou mayest observe to do according to all the law, which Moses my servant commanded thee: turn not from it to the right hand or to the left, that thou mayest prosper whithersoever thou goest. This book of the law shall not depart out of thy mouth; but thou shalt meditate therein day and night, that thou mayest observe to do according to all that is written therein: for then thou shalt make thy way prosperous, and then thou shalt have good success.

Have not I commanded thee? Be strong and of a good courage; be not afraid, neither be thou dismayed: for the Lord thy God is with thee whithersoever thou goest" (Joshua 1:6-9).

God's promises are not meant to set aside His precepts. These Words spoken to Joshua by God were meant to spur him on towards certain victory. The children of Israel were somewhat inexperienced in the art of warfare. Upon entering the land, they would face seven stronger nations who held the land with strongholds and chariots of iron. These words of encouragement and promise would be remembered by Joshua in the midst of heated battles in the months that lay ahead. Joshua was to undertake the task without trepidation or hesitation because the living God had promised that "no man would be able to stand before him..." In the words of Paul the apostle, *"... If God be for us, who can be against us? (Romans 8:31).*

Not only was the land full of numerous and powerful foes, but the people Joshua commanded were faint heart and easily discouraged and ever ready to murmur. Even so, God had promised "I will be with thee..." Preparation goes before possession. Joshua was told to "meditate upon the Word of God." Obedience to the Word of God will dispel all fears and bring courage and prosperity to the faithful. When we are willing to meditate in the Word day and night, we will make our way successful, and enjoy the prosperity God made available to us through His Son Jesus. In I Corinthians 16:13, we are exhorted to *"Watch, stand fast in the faith, quit you like men, be strong."* In Psalm 31:24, we read, *"Be of good courage, and he shall strengthen your heart, all ye that hope in the Lord."*

In the book of Ephesians our walk, warfare, and victory is outlined carefully for us. We read of the warrior's power in Ephesians 6, *"Finally, my brethren, be strong in the Lord, and in the power of his might."* Then we are told to put on the full armor of God. It is a " spiritual armor" with the Word of God as its foundation. Joshua was told to "meditate" and we are told to *"Stand...having your loins girt about with truth...feet shod with the preparation of the gospel of peace...taking the shield of faith, with which ye shall be able to quench all the fiery darts of the wicked."* Full obedience to the precepts of God will cause us to encounter many difficulties; but we have been told to "put on the armor," and fight the good fight of faith. The path of obedience and trust is one of success and prosperity, but we must not turn from it to the left or to the right. But a life of faith calls for a stout heart lest the enemies along the way delight in our destruction.

It was a great and honorable trust which God had lodged into the hands of Joshua. God promised him success, favor and prosperity if he would take the book of the law and devour it; he was to write it on the tables of his heart; keep it close at hand for therein lay his understanding of the task which God had assigned to him. Joshua must observe the law, and see to it that the people did the same. It would not be enough to read and and hear the law, to admire and talk it, but he was commanded to do all that was written therein. Then he would have the victory.

Rahab And The Spies

Joshua took his place as captain of God's people to led them across the Jordan into their long awaited inheritance. He instructed the leaders to tell the people to get ready for they would cross within three days. But the first obstacle in their way was the well-fortified city of Jericho which was only a few miles from the river. Joshua immediately sent forth two men to spy out the land.

The two spies arrived at an inn operated by a harlot named Rahab who had faith in God; she hid the two men from the king's police force in exchange for her household. No more unlikely character could have been chosen to protect these men from arrest than Rahab. She was divinely chosen of God to deliver them; her salvation illustrated that in the midst of impending doom, wicked individuals may find mercy and grace by turning to the Lord God in faith. Lest we find ourselves charging Israel with barbaric cruelty in their manner of warfare, remember as the narrative continues that the inhabitants of the land were their barbaric and idolatrous descendants who not only committed abominations ,but also sought to entice Israel to join them in these "religious" acts. It has been described by the scholars as probably the most depraved religion known to man.[1] *"And the king of Jericho sent unto Rahab, saying, Bring forth the men that are come to thee, which are entered into thine house: for they be come to search out all the country. And the woman took the two men, and hid them, and said thus, There came men unto me, but I wist not whence they were:" (Joshua 2:3,4).*

Every Christian may testify to the fact that the hardest part of entering into our inheritance is the "waiting

---

[1] Religious prostitution, sacrificing of babies, etc.

God." Joshua told the people to wait for three days. After years of weary traveling and waiting, the children of Israel were standing just across from their land, and there remained yet three days to encamp just outside its borders.[2] The waiting, first of all, involved the salvation of a woman and her family. The Sovereign God of the Hebrew people brought His chosen ones to the door of their land, and at the same time, He prepared the heart of a harlot to hunger for His strength and protection. May the Holy Spirit write these spiritual truths on our hearts. There was a soul to be saved before they conquered the land. They had to wait upon the Lord until the time for crossing was right. In Hebrews 11:31, we read more of her faith, *"By faith the harlot Rahab perished not with them that believed not, when she had received the spies with peace."* In James 2:25, we read, *"Likewise also was not Rahab the harlot justified by works, when she had received the messengers, and had sent them out another way?"* Because of her faith, such as it was at the time, Rahab became a part of the blessings God promised to Abraham, Isaac, and Jacob. She became part of the line of the ancestry of Jesus Christ; her works brought about faith, and faith produced the blessings for her and her family.

Judgment would not fall upon wicked Jericho until Rahab was in the kingdom of God. We remember that one righteous man lived in the city of Sodom, and God could do nothing until He was delivered out of the city. In John 4, we have recorded for us the beautiful story of Jesus and the woman at the well. He said that He had a need to go

---

[2]Three days-speaks of Trinity, and Resurrection.

through Samaria. Jesus knew He must take the Good News to a woman who had lived in sin for many years. He said to her, *"...If thou knewest the gift of God, and who it is that saith to thee, Give me to drink: thou wouldest have asked of him, and he would have given thee living water"* (verse 10).

The stories of the miraculous deliverance of the children of God had reached the ears of the men in Jericho, and fear seized their hearts. While God was instructing His Own to "be of good courage," He was devastating the prideful souls of Jericho. A large tribe of Jews were encamped in their back door, and it had been noised all over the land that God was on their side.

"And she said unto the men, I know that the Lord hath given you the land, and that your terror is fallen upon us, and that all the inhabitants of the land faint because of you. for we have heard how the Lord dried up the water of the Red sea for you, when ye came out of Egypt; and what ye did unto the two kings of the Amorites, that were on the other side Jordan, Sihon and Og, whom ye utterly destroyed. And as soon as we had heard these things, our hearts did melt, neither did there remain any more courage in any man, because of you: for the Lord your God, he is God in heaven above, and in earth beneath" (Joshua 2:9-11).

She had hid the spies on the roof of the house in the stalks of flax which she had laid in order there. She told the king's men if they would hurry, it was possible they might overtake the spies. They pursued by way of the Jordan river, and as soon as they set out after the men, the city gates were closed, and the Israelites were locked up inside the walls of Jericho. Rahab had endangered her own life to help the spies. In Psalms 16:7, we read, *"When a man's ways please the Lord, He maketh even his enemies to be at peace with him."*

A Scarlet Cord

Rahab told the men to escape by the wall on which her house was built, and head for the mountains and stay hid for three days. By then the searchers would have returned to the city, and the men would be safe to return to their camp.

Behold, when we come into the land, thou shalt bind this line of scarlet thread in the window which thou didst let us down by: and thou shalt bring thy father, and thy mother, and thy brethren, and all thy father's household, home unto thee. And it shall be that whosoever shall go out of the doors of thy house into the street, his blood shall be upon his head, and we will be guiltless: and whosoever shall be with thee in the house, his blood shall be on our head, if any hand be upon him. And if thou utter this our business, then we will be quit of thine oath, which thou hast made us to swear. And she said, According unto your words, so be it. and she sent them away, and they departed: and she bound the scarlet line in the window" (Joshua 2:18-21).

In the New Testament we read of the Philippian jailor who cried out, *"Sirs, what must I do to be saved?"* And Paul said, *"Believe on the Lord Jesus Christ, and thou shalt be saved, and thy house"* (Acts 16:30,31). There was great rejoicing in his household that night as they received the Lord Jesus and were baptised. We note that when Rahab spoke to the spies about their God she did not say "maybe" or "perhaps" but she said , "I know that the Lord hath given you the land..." When the Lord led the children of Israel from Egypt, they were instructed to put the Blood upon the door posts of their houses, and when the death angel passed over at midnight, all who remained inside were protected by the Blood. This speaks to us of the beautiful salvation of our Lord God through the shed Blood of the Lamb.

The spies gave Rahab a scarlet cord, and told her they would be responsible for only those who were within her walls. They were sheltered by the red cord in her window.[3] In all of Jericho God found one faithful woman through which to save an entire family, and conquer a city.Jesus Christ is our token and surety for all things in this life and life eternal. The truth of the scarlet cord runs from Genesis to the end of the book of Revelation, when the redeemed will sing that song in heaven. But that song must be learned while we are here on this earth.

The Crossing of the Jordan

"And Joshua rose early in the morning; and they removed from Shittim, and came to the Jordan, he and all the children of Israel, and lodged there before they passed over. And it came to pass after three days, that the officers went through the host; And they commanded the people, saying, When ye see the ark of the covenant of the Lord your God, and the priests the Lev-

---
[3] The scarlet cord was for "identification," and for a "token."

ites bearing it, then ye shall remove from your place, and go after it. Yet there shall be a space between you and it, about two thousands cubits by measure; come not near unto it, that ye may know the way by which ye must go; for ye have not passed this way heretofore. And Joshua said unto the people, Sanctify yourselves; for tomorrow the Lord will do wonders among you. And Joshua spoke unto the priests, saying, Take up the ark of the covenant, and pass over before the people. And they took up the ark of the covenant, and went before the people" (Joshua 3:1- 6).

God's timing is always right. They were about to enter the land; but the Jordan waters would have to be passed over. Jordan speaks of death, and the passage of the Jordan is a figure of our death with Christ. Out of judgment and death comes new life. This part of the story of the children of Israel is perhaps one of the most memorable in all their history; while they camped on the banks of the Jordan, instructions came that as soon as they saw the priests carrying the Ark, they were to follow. They were to stay at least half a mile behind the Ark, and no closer; they were to sanctify themselve for the next day God would work wonders among them. They were assured that they could depend upon the Ark (the Lord God) to lead them across the river. So it is with us today; we are assured through the written Word that the Lord Jesus is the Ark, and He will abundantly supply our every need and delights in the desires of our heart. In Psalm 37:23, we read, *"The steps of a good man are ordered by the Lord: and he delighteth in his way."* They prepared to cross the Jordan before they knew how this would be accomplished. Joshua had continued to meditate in the Word day and night, and he trusted the Lord to provide the way as they stepped out in faith to follow the Ark.[4]

We must remember at this point that because of the unbelief of the children of Israel, God caused them to wander on the outskirts of the Land of Promise until all that unbelieving generation had died in the wilderness without realizing the blessings He had in store for them.

Upon entering the land, it is clear that the Pillar of Cloud and the fire that had led them in their wilderness experience was withdrawn, and the "Ark of the Covenant of the Lord," which was in their midst would now take the lead.

"And the Lord said unto Joshua, This day will I begin to magnify thee in the sight of all Israel, that they may know that, as I was with Moses, so I will be with thee. And thou shalt command the priests that bear the ark of the covenant, saying, When ye are come to the brink of the water of Jordan, ye shall stand still in Jordan" (Joshua 3:7,8).

God told Joshua that this was the day in which He would bestow great honor and favor upon him so that all Israel would know that He was with him just as surely as He was with Moses. Joshua delivered God's Words to the people to encourage them as they prepared to cross over the Jordan River. They were to put their total trust in the Lord, for He had promised to deliver them from the hand

---

[4]The meeting place between God and man. The wood of the ark spoke of His perfect humanity; the gold of His Deity.

of the seven nations in Canaan who were His enemies. God is ever willing to prove that He can be trusted. He will carry the lamb in His arms until it is well able to walk. *"He shall feed his flock like a shepherd: He shall gather the lambs with his arm, and carry them in his bosom, and shall gently lead those that are with young" (Isaiah 40:11).* He will give power to the faint hearted, and increase their strength in the day of troubles. When we wait upon the Lord, He has promised that we shall run and not be weary. Joshua was to be rewarded for his trust in the Lord. When we read, *"This day will I begin to magnify thee..."* we are reminded of One infinitely superior to Joshua; what God did here for Joshua His servant, was but a foreshadowment of what later He did for His Son at this same Jordan. Right after Jesus was baptised in the the River Jordan, heaven gave witness of Him. *"Lo, the heavens were opened unto Him and he saw the Spirit of God descending like a dove, and lighting upom Him: And lo, a voice from heaven, saying, This is My beloved Son, in whom I am well pleased" (Matthew 3:16,17).* Then He was *"made manifest to Israel" (John 1:31).* Then was He set forth for His great mission upon this earth; Then did God "begin to magnify Him." We must next observe at what point in the Jordan all this occurred. *"These things were done in Beth-arba" (John 1:28),* which signified *"the place of passage" (John 1:28),* thus we note that Christ was magnified by the Father at the very place where Israel passed through the river and where Joshua was magnified! By what happened at the Jordan, Israel knew that Joshua was their Divinely appointed leader and governor, and they reverenced him all the days of his life. How solemn indeed was the contrast.

Joshua was instructed by God to command the priest, "...When ye are come to the brink of the water of Jordan, ye shall stand still in Jordan." Joshua was to be magnified before the Lord and the people, and he exercised his high authority immediately by giving orders to the priests. We simply note here that just as the priests of Israel must order their actions by instructions received from God to Joshua, so must we who are ministers and priests upon the earth get our orders from the Captain of our Salvation. The priests carrying the Ark were instructed to "...stand still in the Jordan." This was a testing of their faith and obedience to the Word of the Lord. In Isaiah 43:2, we read, *"When thou passest through the waters, I will be with thee; and through the rivers, they shall not overflow thee: when thou walkest through the fire, thou shalt not be burned; neither shall the flame kindle upon thee."* The Lord would not appoint them to go anywhere but where He would go before them to make all their paths straight.

"Behold, the ark of the covenant of the Lord of all the earth passeth over before you into Jordan. Now therefore take you twelve men out of the tribes of Israel, out of every tribe a man. And it shall come to pass, as soon as the soles of the feet of the priests that bear the ark of the Lord, the Lord of all the earth, shall rest in the waters of Jordan, that the waters of Jordan shall be cut off from the waters that come down from above; and it shall stand upon a heap. And it came to pass, when the people removed from their tents, to pass over Jordan, and the priests bearing the ark of the covenant before the people; And as they that bare the ark were come unto Jordan, and the feet of the priests that bare the ark were

dipped in the brim of the water, (for Jordan overfloweth all his banks all the time of harvest,) That the waters which came down from above stood and rose up upon an heap very far from the city Adam, that is beside Zaretan: and those that came down toward the sea of the plain, even the salt sea, failed, and were cut off: and the people passed over right against Jericho. And the priests that bare the ark of the covenant of the Lord stood firm on dry ground in the midst of Jordan, and all the Israelites passed over on dry ground, until all the people were passed clean over Jordan" (Joshua 3:11-17).

The crossing of Jordan was intended to be to the Hebrew people a sure token of God's presence with them, and a sure pledge of their conquest of Canaan. We must be careful to note that they faced conflict in the land, but victory had already been assured. This proves to be a perfect analogy of the warfare of every born again Christian today. Constantly we are reminded that in our daily Christian walk we *"wrestle not against flesh and blood, but against principalities, against powers, against the rulers of the darkness of this world, against spiritual wickedness in high places" (Ephesians 6:12).* We are commanded to stand with our loins girt about with Truth, claiming our right standing with the Lord Jesus Christ.

Attention must be drawn to the fact that in verse 11 and verse 13, God is called, *"the Lord of all the earth,"* which at once intimates it is a statement of special importance. This title is not found in the Pentateuch, but occurs here in Joshua 3 for the first time. It signifies His absolute sovereignty and universal dominion. Certainly Jordan's flood could not keep God from leading His children to possess their possessions. The iniquity of the people was full, and God was ready to act on behalf of His promise to Abraham. But between the promise and its fulfillment flowed the Jordan River which had to be crossed.

The priests were to proceed to the edge of the water then stop. This was to give witness that the Jordan waters were driven back at the presence of the Lord. As Matthew Henry wrote, "God could have divided the river without the priests, but they could not without Him." At this point, attention must be centered upon the Ark of the Lord - the presence of God. Early in the morning the priests took the Ark on their shoulders and marched towards the river which was in its flooding season. As the children of Israel watched , the priests put their feet in the edge of the water and suddenly the waters began piling up against an invisible wall. The priests who were carrying the Ark stood on dry ground in the middle of the Jordan River and waited as all the people passed to the other side near the city of Jericho.

It is both interesting and instructive to consider the many points of contrast and comparison between the parting of the Red Sea and the parting of the Jordan River. The parting of the Red Sea terminated their bondage, whereas, the parting of the Jordan initiated their entrance into the land of promise. The parting of the Red Sea pictured the Israelites on the run, but the parting of the Jordan waters enabled them to cross over and conquer their enemies. The Red Sea was piled high by a strong east wind from the Lord; the Jordan parted by no such means. However, both miracles were connected with water, witnessed to by the entire nation of Israel. Each miracle was designed to authenticate Israel's leader. Each miracle served to test Israel's faith and obedience. With each miracle, the children of Israel went across dryshod. And each inaugurated a new period in Israel's history.

We quote R. Gosse at this point, who so vividly pictured this crossing of the Jordan: "At any time the passage of the river by such a multitude, with their wives and children, their flocks and herds, and all their baggage, would have presented formidable difficulties; but now the channel was filled with a deep and impetuous torrent, which overflowed its banks and spread widely on either side, probably extending nearly a mile in width; while in the very sight of the scene were the Canaanitish hosts, who might be expected to pour out from their fortress and exterminate the invading multitude before they could reach the shore. Yet these difficulties were nothing to Almighty power, and only serve to heighten the effect of the stupendous miracle about to be wrought. No sooner had the feet of the priests touched the brim of the overflowing river than the swollen waters receded from them; and not only the broad lower valley but the deep bed of the stream was presently emptied of water, and its pebbly bottom became dry. The waters which had been in the channel speedily ran off, while those which would naturally have replaced them from above were miraculously suspended, and accumulated in a glassy heap, far above the city Adam...nearly the whole channel of the lower Jordan from a little below the Lake of Tiberias to the Dead Sea was dry."

Two Memorials

Twelve men were appointed earlier for a special task. When all the people were safely across the river, the Lord told Joshua to command each of the twelve men chosen to take a stone from where the priests were standing in the middle of the Jordan, and to carry them out to the place where they would camp that night.

"And Joshua said unto them, Pass over before the ark of the Lord your God into the midst of Jordan, and take you every man of you a stone upon his shoulder, according unto the number of the tribes of the children of Israel: That this may be a sign among you, that when your children ask their fathers in time to come, saying, What mean ye by these stones? Then ye shall answer them, That the waters of Jordan were cut off before the ark of the covenant of the Lord; when it passed over Jordan, the waters of Jordan were cut off: and these stones shall be for a memorial unto the children of Israel for ever" (Joshua 4:5-7).

The men did all that Joshua commanded; they carried the stones to Gilgal where the children of Israel set up camp west of Jordan.

"And Joshua set up twelve stones in the midst of Jordan, in the place where the feet of the priests which bare the ark of the covenant stood: and they are there unto this day. For the priests which bare the ark stood in the midst of ordan, until every thing was finished that the Lord commanded Joshua to speak unto the people, according to all that Moses commanded Joshua: and the people hasted and passed over. And it came to pass, when all the people were clean passed over,. that the ark of the Lord passesd over, and the priests, in the presence of the people. Ands the children of Reuben, and the children of Gad, and half the tribe of Manasseh,

passed over armed before the children of Israel, ans Moses spake unto them: About forty thousand prepared for war passed over before the Lord unto battle, to the plains of Jericho. On that day the Lord magnified Joshua in the sight of all Israel; and they feared him, as they feared Moses, all the days of his life" (Joshua 4:9-14).

These stones were not left flat on the ground, but were raised as a memorial to the miracle at the Jordan; The Hebrew word for "pitch" is defined in Young's Concordance as, "To cause to stand, raise." It is the same word that was used in connection with the erection of the Tabernacle when it was completed. We should note that these stones were stacked in such a way as to cause those who would later pass that way to inquire as to their meaning. And we are told that Joshua set up twelve stones in the midst of Jordan, and there they are to this day. Around the area of that memorial, our Lord Jesus was baptised and anointed for His earthly ministry.

When the people were completely passed over the Jordan, every last one of them, God gave another command to Joshua. It was that the priests bearing the Ark were to come out of the Jordan River. When the priests brought the Ark forth out of the water, and their feet touched the dry ground , the waters of Jordan returned and overflowed the banks as before. This miracle took place the 10th day of the first month.[5] That was the day that the entire nation of Israel, the chosen of God, crossed

---

[5] Five days before their forty years of wandering ended, God brought them into Canaan that they should enter four days before the annual solemnity of the passover, and on the very day when the preparation for it was to begin (Exodus 12:3).

over the Jordan River on a dry bed, and set up camp in Gilgal, at the eastern edge of the city of Jericho around their memorial of twelve stones taken from the river bed.

The twelve stones set in the river bed speaks of the mercy and infinite grace of God that He bestowed upon us through the finished work of the Lord Jesus Christ at Calvary. He died for us and now we are dead to this world and its ways. Sin shall have no dominion over us, and we reckon ourselves dead indeed to sin, and resurrected to a new life in Him. In Colossians 3:1, we read, *"If ye then be risen with Christ, seek those things which are above, where Christ sitteth on the right hand of God."* We must take our place in baptism with Him. Jordan represented the river of death, but the children of God crossed over dry shod. Death holds no power over the born-again child of God. Down in the waters to identify with His death, but up again to walk in the newness of life with Him.

Circumcision

Circumcision was the sign of the Abrahamic Covenant. During the later years of the Egyptian bondage, this separating sign had been neglected; and this disobedience to God's command continued throughout the wilderness wanderings.[6] This symbolizes the Christian of today who conforms to this world, and fails to crucify the deeds of the flesh.

"And this is the cause why Joshua did circumcise: All the people that came out of Egypt, that were males,

---

[6]The key to Joshua 5 is found in Numbers 14, Dadesh-barnea

even all the men of war, died in the wilderness by the way, after they came out of Egypt. Now all the people that came out were circumcised: but all the people that were born in the wilderness by the way as they came forth out of Egypt, them they had not circumcised. For the children of Israel walked forty years in the wilderness, till all the people that were men of war, which came out of Egypt, were consumed, because they obeyed not the voice of the Lord: unto whom the Lord sware that he would not show them the land, which the Lord sware unto their fathers that he would give us, a and that floweth with milk and honey. And their children, whom he raised up in their stead, them Joshua circumcised: for they were uncircumcised, because they had not circumcised them by the way. And it came to pass, when they had done circumcising all the people, that they abode in their places in the camp, till they were whole. And the Lord said unto Joshua, This day have I rolled away the reproach of Egypt from off you. Wherefore the name of the place is called Gilgal unto this day" (Joshua 5:4-9).

We must never assume that we are ready for battle until we wave taken the knife of the Word to our heart. This sharp knife speaks to us of self-judgment. This rite of circumcision of old was designed by God to mark off His people from the ungodly people around them. It was a sign of separation, and typified death to the flesh. When Stephen was being stoned, he cried out, *"Ye stiffnecked and uncircumcised in heart and ears, ye do always resist the Holy Ghost: as your fathers did, so do you" (Acts 7:51).*

In Romans 2:29, Paul said, *"...and circumcision is that of the heart."* In Jeremiah 4:4, we read, *"Circumcise yourselves to the Lord, and take away the foreskins of your heart..."*

Gilgal

"And the children of Israel encamped in Gilgal, and kept the passover on the fourteenth day of the month at even in the plains of Jericho. And they did eat of the old corn of the land on the morrow after the passover, unleavened cakes, and parched corn in the selfsame day. And the manna ceased on the morrow after they had eaten of the old corn of the land;' neither had the children of Israel manna any more; but they did eat of the fruit of the land of Canaan that year" (Joshua 5:10-12).

Manna was wilderness food; it had been provided by God at that time to meet the needs of His people. But now they were to feed from the "fat of the land."

Passover

The passover had been observed only twice before. Once, when the Israelites went out of Egypt lead by Moses, the servant of God, and the other time at Mount Sinai. Since God had commanded that no uncircumcised person partake of the passover, it had been abandoned altogether, (Exodus 12:48). They had forfeited their privileges and blessings by living in disobedience and unbelief. This is a lesson that applies to all of us today. There can never be any feasting on the Lord in our hearts, or any real worship to the Father, if we harbor doubt and unbelief or live in wilful sin. There will be no "passover feast" until the heart is made right with its Creator. Sin separates us from God. Paul admonishesd us to examine our own lives lest we drink of the "cup" unworthily; to eat and drink of the "Lord's Supper" unworthily often results in sickness and premature death.

The act of circumcision and the keeping of the passover were both acts of obedience towards God at Gilgal; one act could not be performed without the other. It was also an act of commemoration to the Sovereign God Who had led them out of bondage, and brought them to this place. The passover was observed with great anticipation for they were about to possess their possessions.

Captain Of The Host

"And it came to pass, when Joshua was by Jericho, that he lifted up his eyes and looked, and behold, there stood a man over against him with his sword drawn in his hand: and Joshua went unto him, and said unto him, Art thou for us, or for our adversaries? And he said, Nay; but as captain of the host of the Lord am I now come. And Joshua fell on his face to the earth, and did worship, and said unto him, What saith my lord unto his servant? And the captain of the Lord's host said unto Joshua, Loose thy shoe from off thy foot; for the place whereon thou standest is holy. And Joshua did so" (Joshua 5:13-15).

While Joshua was checking out the city of Jericho, a man appeared nearby with drawn sword. Joshua was not afraid. He went over to him and ask if He were friend or foe. God has promised to honor those who honor Him, and Joshua had been faithful in the circumcising of the people, and in the keeping of the passover and the feast of the unleaven bread. In John 14:21, we read, *"He that hath My commandments and keepeth them, he it is that loveth me: and he that loveth me shall be loved of my Father, and I will love him and will manifest myself to him."*

We note that the token of reverence required of Joshua was also required of Moses at the burning bush, where God spoke and commissioned him to go to Pharaoh and speak in behalf of His children in bondage there (Exodus 3). As Joshua fell on his face before Him, he asked for directions. His first instructions to Joshua were for him to take off his shoes for he was upon Holy ground. In this Joshua obeyed, and waited for his orders.

Chapter 2

CONQUERING THE LAND

"Now Jericho was straitly shut up because of the children of Israel: none went out, and none came in. And the Lord said unto Joshua, See, I have given into thine hand Jericho, and the king thereof, and the mighty men of valour. And ye shall compass the city, all ye men of war, and go around about the city once. Thus shalt thou do six days. And seven priests shall bear before the ark seven trumpets of rams' horns: and the seventh day ye shall compass the city seven times, and the priests shall blow with the trumpets. And it shall come to pass, that when they make a long blast with the rams' horn, and when ye hear the sound of the trumpet, all the people shall shout with a great shout; and the wall of the city shall fall down flat, and the people shall ascend up every man straight before him" (Joshua 6:1-5).

The Siege and Fall of Jericho

The fall of Jericho is the most interesting and probably the most instructive incident recorded in the book of Joshua. The gates of the city were tightly shut against those "peculiar" people camped near the river.

They were afraid of the Israelites, and no one ventured outside the walls of the city. But the Canaanites would have to be dispossessed before Israel could settle down in peace in the land. Here we behold how very different the ways of God from ours, and how futile are the efforts of those who oppose His plan.

God's instructions were implicit. There was no room for the "wisdom" of man, or military strategy; God told Joshua that He had given them Jericho, and the king, and the mighty men of valour which left no place for the boastings of man. The men of war were to march around the city once a day for six days followed by seven priests walking ahead of the Ark, each carrying a trumpet made from a ram's horn. On the seventh day they were instructed to walk around the city seven times while the priests blew the trumpets. They were to move in total silence until the moment Joshua bid them shout.

The blowing of the trumpets would strike terror in the hearts of the Canaanites, but it would encourage the people of God. For six days this strange procession continued; but on the seventh day they rose about the dawning of the day and compassed the city seven times - the priests blew the trumpets - and Joshua said, *"SHOUT! for the Lord hath given you the city!"* The walls of Jericho fell and the children of Israel entered and destroyed the city. Joshua had instructed the men not to harm Rahab for she had protected their spies. Though they burned and destroyed everything in the city, the young spies brought out Rahab and her entire household. Arrangements were made for them to live with the Israelites outside the city.

Joshua adjured the elders of Israel that Jericho was condemned to a perpetual desolation, and a curse was pronounced upon the man that at any time thereafter should offer to rebuild it. God would have the city to remain in ruins as a constant reminder of His wrath against His enemies, and as a token of His love and mercy for His Own people. This curse did come upon a man who long after rebuilt Jericho. Hiel, a man from Bethel, rebuilt Jericho. As he laid the foundations, his oldest son died; when he finally completed the task, his youngest son died (I Kings 16:34).

Sin In The Camp

"But the children of Israel committed a trespass in the accursed thing: for Achan, the son of Carmi, the son of Zabdi, the son of Serah, of the tribe of Judah, took of the accursed thing: and the anger of the Lord was kindled against the children of Israel. And Joshua sent men from Jericho to Ai, which is beside Beth-aven, on the east side of Beth-el, and spake unto them, saying, Go up and view the country. And the men went up and viewed Ai. And they returned to Joshua, and said unto him, Let not all the people go up; but let about two or three thousand men go up and smite Ai; and make not all the people to labour thither; for they are but few. So they went up thither of the people about three thousand men: and they fled before the men of Ai. And the men of Ai smote

of them about thirty and six men: for they chased them from before the gate even unto Shebarim, and smote them in the going down: wherefore the hearts of the people melted, and became as water" (Joshua 7:1-5).

The taking of Jericho was an easy win; the next fortress to be taken was Ai. It seems that the country was broken up into small territories, each under an independent king. Ai was situated upon a hill about ten miles to the west of Jericho, and was about 12,000 population. Its location was exceedingly important, and Joshua deemed it of utmost importance to send out men to view the city.

In Joshua 6:18, we read that Joshua warned the people not to take any of the loot from the city for it was cursed, and had to be totally destroyed; he warned that if anyone took of the accursed things, the entire nation would answer to God. The silver, gold, utensils of bronze, and the iron would be dedicated to the Lord, and brought into His treasury. We note something is amiss when we read in Joshua 7:1, *"But the children of Israel committed a trespass in the accursed thing...Achan...of the tribe of Judah, took of the accursed thing..."* Thus far their story had been one of victory and favor over their enemies; but here we find them in full retreat, and 36 men were killed because one man and his family failed to obey the commandments of the Lord. Sin in the camp caused the innocent to suffer the loss of their loved ones.

It is most important for us to note that the sin of Israel which led to defeat at Ai was the deliberate disobedience of Achan, for God held the entire nation corporately responsible, and caused their hearts to melt within them as they presumptuously entered into battle without consulting the Lord. Since they saw the city was small, they sent forth only a few men.

God looked upon the twelve tribes of Israel as one unit; they formed one nation, and what affected one part, or tribe, affected all. Though they were divided later, the book of James addresses them as a whole.

A Penitent Leader's Prayer

"And Joshua rent his clothes, and fell to the earth upon his face before the Ark of the Lord until the eventide, he and the elders of Israel, and put dust upon their heads. And Joshua said, Alas, O Lord God, wherefore hast thou at all brought this people over Jordan, to deliver us into the hand of the Amorites, to destroy us? would to God we had been content, and dwelt on the other side Jordan! O Lord, what shall I say, when Israel turneth their backs before their enemies! for the Canaanites and all the inhabitants of the land shall hear of it, and shall environ us round, and cut off our name from the earth: and what wilt thou do unto thy great name (Joshua 7:6-9)?

Joshua and the elders prostrated themselves before the Ark of the Lord, and tore their clothing; there they lay all day until the evening with dust upon their heads to demonstrate their sore anguish over their losses. How easy it is for Christians who have suffered losses and faced seemingly unsurmountable odds in life to blame the Lord, and question His integrity. Had not Joshua been instructed at the very outset of his mission to seek the Lord at all times? He was warned to mediate in the Word day and night, yet we see he went into battle without first asking of the Lord. God knew that Joshua would need a triple amount of courage to lead the children of Israel into the land He had promised to them. Joshua had been warned to be strong in the Lord and not lean to his own ways. This serves as an example of what happens when we listen to the carnal counsel of men instead of seeking the widom of the Lord God from the Word. This act of disobedience on his part caused him to fall on his face like a sobbing child blaming God for their troubles. As their leader, Joshua likely concerned himself over the fact that failure at this point reflected upon his own ability.

This story and its final outcome is absolute proof to the Christian that God has provided victory, and He makes no provision for sin. The saint of God need not live in defeat. But the devil is a wily creature, and seeks whom he may devour. He was as much at work with the children of Israel as he is with the born-again today. How blessed we are to have the Holy Spirit Who lives within and guides us step by step.

Practical Lesson

Another practical lesson to be learned from this Biblical incident in connection with "possessing our possessions" is that when God has revealed precious truths to us from His Word, and delivered us from some vanity or lust in life, we must beware lest we become conceited and attribute the victories to our own ability and cease to be watchful against the spirit of Nebuchadnezzar who said, *"Is not this great Babylon that I have built for the house of the kingdom by the might of my power"* (Dan-

iel 4:30)?" Remember that solemn warning from Deuteronomy 32:15, *"But Jeshurun (Israel) waxed fat and wicked: thou art waxed fat, thou art grown thick, thou art covered with fatness: then he forsook God."* Let us ever be on guard against the Laodicean self-sufficiency and self-glorying of our day.

It is most important to note that the Holy Spirit has given us the genealogy of the offender, and his name is Achan which means "trouble." He was the immediate descendant of Zerah, who was the son of Judah's whoredom mentioned in Genesis 38:15-30.

"And the Lord said unto Joshua, Get thee up; wherefore liest thou thus upon thy face? Israel hath sinned, and they have also transgressed my covenant which I commanded them: for they have even taken of the accursed thing, and have also stolen, and dissembled also, and they have put it even among their own stuff. Therefore the children of Israel could not stand before their enemies, but turned their backs before their enemies, because they were accursed: neither will I be with you any more, except ye destroy the accursed from among you. Up, sanctify the people, and say, Sanctify yourselves against tomorrow: for thus saith the Lord God of Israel, there is an accursed thing in the midst of thee, O Israel: thou canst not stand before thine enemies, until ye take away the accursed thing from among you. In the morning therefore ye shall be brought according to your tribes; and it shall be, that the tribe which the Lord taketh shall come according to the families thereof; and the household which the Lord shall take shall come man by man. and it shall be, that he that is taken with the accursed thing shall be burnt

with fire, he and all that he hath: because he hath transgressed the covenant of the Lord, and because he hath wrought folly in Israel" (Joshua 7:10-15).

Because of sin in the camp, Israel had no power to stand before their enemies. Even in this dispensation of grace, sin in the church can cause it to be weak and sickly and many Christians die before their time. In Hebrews 3:13, we read, *"Take heed, brethren, lest there be in any of you an evil heart of unbelief."*

Joshua cried is heart out before the Lord, and the Lord told him to get up; it was time to act for the children of Israel had sinned and transgressed his covenant. We must carefully note that Joshua and the elders had been on their faces for a while interceding for the nation. Now it was time to get the accursed thing out of the camp and deal with the offenders.

Israel had taken loot, hid it, and lied about it; victory would be withheld until things were made right in the sight of God.

Each one had to undergo purification rites, and on the morrow they were to appear by tribes and the Lord would point out the tribe to which the guilty one belonged; then that tribe would come forward by clans and the Lord would point out the guilty clan to which the offender belonged. Then they would come by families, and the Lord would select the guilty family; and the family that the Lord selected would come one by one until the guilty member was announced.

The Stoning of Achan

In all of this Achan was found to be the guilty one; his sin had caused the children of Israel to run from their enemies, and three thousand lost their lives. Achan confessed that when he saw the beautiful robe imported from Babylon, the silver and gold, he could not resist, so he took the loot and hid it in the ground under his tent where he thought it would be unnoticed.

After some of the men recovered the goods, they took Achan, his family, and all he had, and what he had stolen, to the valley of Achor and there Israel stoned them to death and burned their bodies. It is called to this day the "Valley of Calamity." Judgment against sin is of God. We must remember that sin in the camp will weaken us and hold back God's blessings; but sin judged and dealt with will open the way for the mercies of God to work freely in our lives.

Chapter 3

POSSESSING THE LAND

After Jericho, Ai was the next city which fell before the Israelite conquest. It was east of Bethel. The Israelites were allowed to take spoils of Ai, and thereafter to destroy it. Joshua's first contingent of 3000 were defeated due to the sin of Achan from the tribe of Judah, in the conquest at Jericho. In trhe second attack on Ai, Joshua planned a diversionary offensive with 30,000 men. The king and 12,000 were killed, and the city set ablaze being turned into a heap of ruins.

"And the Lord said unto Joshua, Fear not, neither be thou dismayed: take all the people of war with thee, and arise, go up to Ai: see, I have given into thy hand the king of Ai, and his people, and his city, and his land: And thou shalt do to Ai and her king as thou didst unto

Jericho and her king: only the spoil thereof, and the cattle thereof, shall ye take for a prey unto yourselves: lay thee an ambush for the city behind it" (Joshua 8:1-2).

Ambush

Joshua chose 30,000 men according to the Word of the Lord, and sent them away by night. They were to hide in ambush close behind the city, ready for action. When the main army attacked the city, Joshua planned that as the army of Ai came out to fight, he and his men would run as they had done before, and Ai would think they were too scared to fight.

"And I, and all the people who are with me, will approach unto the city; and it shall come to pass, when they come out against us, as at the first, that we will flee before them (For they will come out after us), till we have drawn them from the city; for they will say, They flee before us, as at the first. Therefore we will flee before them. Then ye shall rise up from the ambush, and seize upon the city: for the Lord your God will deliver it into your hand. And it shall be, when ye have taken the city, that ye shall set the city on fire, according to the commandment of the Lord shall ye do. See, I have commanded you" (Joshua 8:4-8).

In this we note that God's people are never left to their own devices; God will set the ambush against Satan, and invite His children to partake of the victory.

"And there was not a man left in Ai or Beth-el, that went not out after Israel: and they left the city open, and pursued after Israel. And the Lord said unto Joshua, Stretch out the spear that is in thy hand toward Ai; for

I will give it into thine hand. And Joshua stretched out the spear that he had in his hand toward the city. And the ambush arose quickly out of their place, and they ran as soon as he had stretched out his hand: and they entered into the city, and took it, and hasted and set the city on fire. And when the men of Ai looked behind them, they saw, and, behold, the smoke of the city asceneded up to heaven, and they had no power to flee this way or that way: and the people that fled to the wilderness turned back upon the pursuers. and when Joshua and all Israel saw that the ambush had taken the city, and that the smoke of the city ascended, then they turned again, and slew the men of Ai" (Joshua 8:17-21).

They captured the king of Ai, and Joshua hanged him on a tree until evening; then the men took his carcase down and cast it at the entrance of the the gate of the city, and stacked a heap of stones thereon.

Blessings And Cursings Read

"Then Joshua built an altar unto the Lord God of Israel in Mount Ebal, As Moses the servant of the Lord commanded the children of Israel, as it is written in the book of the law of Moses, an altar of whole stones, over which no man hath lift up any iron: and they offered thereon burnt offerings unto the Lord, and sacrificed peace offerings. And he wrote there upon the stones a copy of the law of Moses, which he wrote in the presence of the children of Israel...And afterward he read all the words of the law, the blessings and cursings, according to all that is written in the book of the law. There was

not a word of all that Moses commanded, which Joshua read not before all the congregation of Israel, with the women, and the little ones, and the strangers that were conversant among them" (Joshua 8:30-35)."

This altar was built of whole stones, upon which no tool had been lifted, as Moses had said to them in Exodus 20:25. This altar speaks of Christ. It would not be shaped by man's efforts. The peace offerings and the burnt offerings which were placed upon these altars speak of Christ offering Himself to God without spot in our behalf. After the sacrifices were made, the altar was turned into a monument. The altar was the "meeting place" between God and man.[1]

Led by the Ark of the Covenant of the Lord, the children of Israel marched forward into Canaan to conquer and gain what God had so many centuries before promised to their forefathers. God intended that just the sight of the Israelites would cause the hearts of the nations to tremble; Israel was Divinely appointed to receive the Kingdom of God, and to be His obedient subjects. In this they failed miserably. God intended to make of them a great nation - a wise people - set apart from the rest of the world; yet we read later of how they declared they wanted to be as other people and have an earthly king over them. It was God'd intention that Israel should stand as a witness to all the world. God may have at this moment set aside His chosen, but rest assured He will again deal with them

---

[1] On one side of the lovely valley of Shechem was Mount Ebal, and on the other side was Mount Gerizim. It is a well known fact that one can stand on top of Mount Ebal and speak with someone on top of Mount Gerizim without raising the voice because of the perfect natural acoustics provided by the valley below for the voices ring from peak to peak.

as His Own. One day the nation Israel will understand that He is One God in Three Persons. He can be a Trinity and manifest Himself in different ways to man just as easily as He by His Own Power can cause a rod to turn into a serpent, then back to a rod; just as easily as He can part the Red Sea or still the waters of Jordan; just as easily as He can cause the walls of Jericho to fall at the mere shout of a man. He is God and He can do with us as He choses.

Deception By The Gibeonites

It has been well said that "Satan plays with loaded dice." He knows all of the avenues of the weaknesses of man. He has had hundreds of centuries to deceive and wreck humanity. He is an expert in the "black art" of deception and lies. The great Apostle Paul warned us to be on our guard. We are to keep on the full armour so we can rest in the assurance of our salvation; we are not to be easy prey for the devil by listening to every "sad" report that comes along.

In chapter nine we have a very striking illustration of the deceptive devices of Satan. The word got out that Ai had been totally destroyed, and the king hanged by Joshua; other kings gathered together in one accord to fight against him. All tribal wars among the Canaanites had been set aside; the enemy would now ban together in an all out effort to annihilate that hoard of people coming at them from across the Jordan.

"And when the inhabitants of Gibeon heard what Joshua had done unto Jericho and to Ai, They did work wilily, and went and made as if they had been ambassadors, and took old sacks upon their asses, and wine

bottles, old, and rent, and bound up; And old shoes and clouted upon their feet, and old garments upon them and all the bread of their provision was dry and mouldy. And they went to Joshua unto the camp at Gilgal, and said unto him, and to the men of Israel, We be come from a far country: now therefore make yea league with us. And the men of Israel said unto the Hivites, Peradventure ye dwell among us; and how shall we make a league with you? And they said unto Joshua, We are thy servants. And Joshua said unto them, Who are ye? and from whence come ye? And they said unto him, From a very far country thy servants are come because of the name of the Lord thy God: for we have heard the fame of him, and all that he did in Egypt, And all that he did to the two kings of the Amorites, that were beyond Jordan, to Sihon king of Heshbon, and to Og king of Bashan, which was at Ashtaroth. Wherefore our elders and all the inhabitants of our country spake to us, saying, Take victuals with you for the journey, and go to meet them, and say unto them, We are your servants: therefore now make ye a league with us. This our bread we took hot for our provision out of our houses on the day we came forth to go unto you; but now, behold, it is dry, and it is mouldy: And these bottles of wine, which we filled, were new; and behold, they be rent: and these our garments and our shoes are become old by reason of the very long journey" (Joshua 9:3-13).

This was a very clever ruse on the part of the Hivites; it accomplished its purpose. Joshua and his officers were deceived by their appearance and the sad story they told of their long journey to reach them in safety. To add insult to injury, they pretended to have traveled that distance because of the Lord God. We must keep in mind that the book of Joshua is more than just an historical record of the conquest and occupation of the land of Canaan; indeed, it is a shadowing forth of that spiritual warfare which every Christian experiences. As long as there is sin in the world, there will be conflict in the life of everyone. We must remember that victory and battles line up side by side. The Word of God has promised us the victory in Jesus. The devil *"as a roaring lion"* seeks to destroy us before we can reach our desired goals.

Note that the Gibeonites were clever enough not to mention the defeats at Jericho and Ai for that would have been a dead give-a-way that they had not traveled very far. They spoke only of what they had heard that God had done for His people in the wilderness journey. Satan's intention was to take the children of Israel from within. Perhaps they had spies in their midst at Mount Ebal where the law was read who had brought them word that these people were to make no covenant with the enemy, and give them no mercy in battle; this caused the Canaanites to fear for their lives. Therefore, we must understand this warning that evil comes to us in different disguises. Someone once said that the devil doesn't care what we stand for - he is only interested in what we will fall for. In I John 4:1, we read, *"Beloved, believe not every spirit, but try the spirits whether they are of God: because many false prophets are gone out into the world."* But great encouragement is applied to our heart in I John 4:4, *"Ye are of God, little children, and have overcome them: because greater is he that is in you, than he that is in the world."* Needless to say, many an alliance that has brought ruin to a church, wrecked a home, and brought defeat to a Christian, has begun in just that same way. Many Christians have discovered that things which seemed not to matter so much at the time have been the devil's rod of defeat. We must always test the situation in light of the Word of God.

"And the men took of their victuals, and asked not counsel at the mouth of the Lord. And Joshua made peace with them, and made a league with them, to let them live: and the princes of the congregation sware unto them" (Joshua 9:14-15).

Joshua and his officers did not bother to counsel with the Lord, and they signed a peace treaty with their enemy, and we are told that the leaders of Israel ratified this agreement with a binding oath. Three days later the sad facts were revealed. These men were close neighbors; but they had signed a treaty and the oath could not be broken. They had to spare their lives. Therefore, they became servants to Israel: carrying the water and chopping the wood.

Sun, Stand Thou Still

"And the Lord said unto Joshua, Fear them not: for I have delivered them into thine hand; there shall not a man of them stand before thee. Joshua therefore came unto them suddenly, and went up from Gilgal all night. And the Lord discomfited them before Israel, and slew them with a great slaughter at Gibeon, and chased them along the way that goeth up to Beth-horon, and smote them to Azekah, and unto Makkedah. And it came to pass, as they fled from before Israel, and were in the going down to Beth-horon, that the Lord cast down

great stones from heaven upon them unto Azekah, and they died: they were more which died with hailstones than they whom the children of Israel slew with the sword. Then spake Joshua to the Lord in the day when the Lord delivered up the Amorites before the children of Israel, and he said in the sight of Israel, Sun, stand thou still upon Gibeon; and thou, Moon, in the valley of Ajalon. And the sun stood still, and the moon stayed, until the people had avenged themselves upon their enemies. Is not this written in the book of Jasher? So the sun stood still in the midst of heaven, and hasted not to go down about a whole day. And there was no day like that before it or after it, that the Lord hearkened unto the voice of a man: for the Lord fought for Israel" (Joshua 10:8-14).

Gibeon was a great city, and when the other nations or territories heard that they had made peace with Israel, they formed a confederation, headed by Adonizedek, king of Jerusalem, and set out to attack Gibeon as a warning to the other districts not to do the same.

The men of Gibeon quickly sent word for Joshua and his men to come help them. The Lord spoke to Joshua as he prepared to enter battle to help Gibeon. How often have we read these encouraging words of *"Fear not - I have won the victory for you."* As the enemy fled with Israel pursuing, panic overtook the other Canaanites and they did not attempt a united stand against the God of the Hebrews. It was then that Joshua uttered his prayer to the Lord, and said in the sight of all Israel, *"Sun, stand thou still upon Gibeon; and thou, Moon, in the valley of Ajalon."* Skeptics have sneered at this ever down through the centuries; just what really took place we may not fully understand, but we do know that the sun stood still and the moon stayed, as Joshua commanded. It was the miracle of miracles performed by God in the sight of His people and recorded as fact in the written Word of God by One Who is Superior to all laws whether of man or nature.

Victory At Makkedah

Joshua and the Israeli army returned to Gilgal. During the battle five kings had hid in a cave, and when news of this reached Captain Joshua, he commanded that a large stone be rolled over the front of the cave to keep them in. Then he sent out orders for the men to continue destroying their enemies for the Lord God was with them. When they returned to their camp at Makkedah, Joshua had the men remove the stone and bring out the kings. He told the captains of his army to put their feet on the necks of the kings as an example of what all God would do for them as He fought for them against their enemies. Joshua plunged a sword into the heart of each king; then he hanged them on five trees until the evening. As the sun was setting, Joshua instructed his men to take the bodies and cast them into the cave where the men had been hiding. Their hiding place became their grave. Joshua totally destroyed the city. Next, they went to Libnah; there God gave them the city and its king.

From Libnah they went to Lachish and attacked and took the city. They captured Eglon on their first day of attack, and killed all its inhabitants as before. From Eglon they moved on to Hebron and captured it and all the surrounding villages, slaughtering the entire population. On to Debir they marched and conquered it quickly. Joshua and his army conquered the whole country as God had promised for the Lord God was with the Hebrew people.

Northern Palestine

"And when all these kings were met together, they came and pitched together at the waters of Merom, to fight against Israel. And the Lord said unto Joshua, Be not afraid because of them: for tomorrow about this time will I deliver them up all slain before Israel: thou shalt hough their horses, and burn their chariots with fire" (Joshua 11:5).

All the kings united to crush Israel, but the Lord God was their Captain of War. He had promised Israel the land, and they would take it at all cost. Again the Lord spoke to Joshua not to be afraid of the people in the land.

"So Joshua took the whole land according to all that the Lord said unto Moses; and Joshua gave it for an inheritance unto Israel according to their divisions by their tribes. And the land rested from war" (Joshua 11:23).

Caleb Received Hebron

Men from the tribe of Judah, led by Caleb, came to Joshua in Gilgal to remind him of Caleb's portion. Caleb was eighty-five years old, and declared himself to be as strong as he was when he spied out the land under the leadership of Moses. He asked for the hill country which the Lord God promised him. So Joshua blessed him and gave him Hebron because he had followed the Lord God of Israel. Caleb had in a sense said, "Give me my mountain; I have conquered.

"Hebron therefore became the inheritance of Caleb the son of Jephunneh the Kenezite unto this day, be-

cause that he wholly followed the Lord God of Israel. And the name of Hebron before was Kirjath-arba; which Arba was a great man among the Anakims. And the land had rest from war" (Joshua 14:14-15).

Tabernacle At Shiloh

Shiloh was situated in the tribal allotment of Ephraim. It was built on a hill about nine miles north of Bethel; it had a commanding and somewhat central location. We find the tabernacle was temporarily located there.

"And the whole congregation of the children of Israel assembled together at Shiloh, and set up the tabernacle of the congregation there. And the land was subdued before them" (Joshua 18:1).

Six Cities Of Refuge

Then Joshua asked the children of Israel how long they would wait before conquering the rest of Canaan. Much of the rest of the book of Joshua is given to tribal allotments, but we will view the six cities of refuge as a type of our Lord Jesus Christ Who is the strong tower to us.

"The Lord also spake unto Joshua, saying, Speak to the children of Israel, saying, Appoint out for you cities of refuge, whereof I spake unto you by the hand of Moses: That the slayer that killeth any person unawares and unwittingly may flee thither: and they shall be your refuge from the avenger of blood. And when he that doth flee unto one of those cities shall stand at the en-

tering of the gate of the city, and shall declare his cause in the ears of the elders of that city, they shall take him into the city unto them, and give him a place, that he may dwell among them. And if the avenger of blood pursue after him, then they shall not deliver the slayer up into his hand; because he smote his neighbour unwittingly, and hated him not beforetime. And he shall dwell in that city, until he stand before the congregation for judgment, and until the death of the high priest that shall be in those days: then shall the slayer return, and come unto his own city, and unto his own house, unto the city from whence he fled" (Joshua 20:1-6).

This is a list of Cities chosen as the cities of refuge for the innocent slayer:

(1) Kedesh of Galilee in the hill country of Naphtali;

(2) Shechem in the hill country of Ephraim;

(3) Kiriath-arba (Hebron) in the hill country of Judah;

(4) Bezer in the wilderness of the land of the tribe of Reuben;

(5) Ramoth of Gilead, tribe of Gad;

(6) Golan of Bashan, tribe of Manasseh.

As H.A. Ironsides suggested, it is very evident that God has hidden some special lessons for us in the types of the Cities of Refuge. In four other passages the Spirit of God drew the attention of Israel to the importance of these cities. First, we have it but briefly mentioned in Exodus 21:13, promising Israel that when they reached the land, He would provide such a refuge; then, in Numbers 35:6, 9-28, He told them that among provide such a refuge; then in Numbers 35:6, 9-28, He told them that among the cities given to the Levites would be six cities of refuge; and Deuteronomy 4:41-43, and 19:1-10, with our present text. Matthew Henry wrote, "These cities (as those also on the other side Jordan) stood in the three several parts of the country, so conveniently that a man might (they say) in half a day reach some one of them from any corner of the country. God is a refuge at hand...They were Levites' cities, which put an honour upon God's tribe, making them judges in those cases wherein divine Providence was so nearly concerned, and protectors to oppressed innocency."

These cities were on a hill for a city on a hill cannot be hid. This would both direct and encourage the poor man making his way to safety. Many observe the connection between the names of these cities, and Christ our refuge: Kedesh signifies holy, and Jesus Christ the Holy One of God is made unto believers sanctification as well as righteousness (I Corinthians 1:30); In the Redeemer we have a sanctuary of Holiness. Shechem, shoulder, which is the place of strength (Isaiah 9:7), and of safety (Luke 15:5). Under the government of Jesus we find our safety and help. Hebron, fellowship, and believers are called into fellowship with the Lord Jesus Christ; Bezer, a fortification, for he is a stronghold to all who trust in him (Nahum 1:7); Ramoth, high or exalted, for in Christ we are elevated above the world, and made to sit in heavenly places (Ephesians 2). Golan, joy or exaltation, for we also joy in God through our Lord Jesus Christ (Romans 5:11).

There was no refuge offered to one who was guilty of wanton and wilful murder. To prevent any guilty one taking advantage of this provision for the innocent, the accused was required by God's law to stand before the congregation in judgment. He would then be given a fair trial.

Hidden so beautifully in this command of God, is a blessed type of the Lord Himself making provision for His people through the shed blood of His Son Jesus Christ. All have sinned and come short of the glory of God. All mankind stands guilty of the death of His Son. The manslayer stayed in the city of refuge until after the death of the high priest; then he was free to return to his home. Christ is not only the One slain and the very city of refuge itself, but He is the High Priest, and as such He will never die again. He is an everlasting priesthood; so those who seek refuge in Him will be eternally safe. On the cruel Roman cross, our Lord settled the sin question; He put all mankind on the ground of manslaughter instead of murder when He prayed for those who had been so adamant in rejecting Him. From His place of death, He cried out, *"Father, forgive them."* God opened for us a city of refuge in His Son when we run to Him and asked forgiveness. The gates into the city of refuge were always open, and no one was turned away.

The Last Days Of Joshua

"And it came to pass a long time after that the Lord had given rest unto Israel from all their enemies round about, that Joshua waxed old and stricken in age. And Joshua called for all Israel, and for their elders, and for their heads, and for their judges, and for their officers and said unto them, I am old and stricken in age: And

ye have seen all that the Lord your God hath done unto all these nations because of you; for the Lord your God is he that hath fought for you. Behold, I have divided unto you by lot these nations that remain, to be an inheritance for your tribes, from Jordan, with all the nations that I have cut off, even unto the great sea westward. And the Lord your God, he shall expel them from before you, and drive them from out of your sight; and ye shall possess their land, as the Lord your God hath promised unto you. Be ye therefore very courageous to keep and to do all that is written in the book of the law of Moses, that ye turn not aside therefrom to the right hand or to the left; That ye come not among these nations, these that remain among you; neither make mention of the name of their gods, nor cause to swear by them, neither serve them, nor bow yourselves unto them. But cleave unto the Lord your God, as ye have done unto this day. For the Lord hath driven out from before you great nations and strong: but as for you, no man hath been able to stand before you unto this day. One of you shall chase a thousand: for the Lord your God, he it is that fighteth for you, as he hath promised. Take good heed therefore unto yourselves, that ye love the Lord your God. Else if ye do in any wise go back, and cleave unto the remnant of these nations, even these that remain among you, and shall make marriages with them, and go in unto them, and they to you: Know for a certainty that the Lord your God will no more drive out any of these nations from before you; but they shall be snares and traps unto you, and scourges in your sides, and thorns in your eyes, until ye perish from off this good land which the Lord your

God hath given you. And, behold, this day I am going the way of all earth: and ye know in all your hearts and in all your souls, that not one thing hath failed of all the good things which the Lord your God spake concerning you; all are come to pass unto you, and not one thing hath failed thereof. Therefore it shall come to pass, that as all good things are come unto you, which the Lord your God promised you; so shall the Lord bring upon you all evil things, until he have destroyed you from off this good land which the Lord your God hath given you. When ye have transgressed the covenat of the Lord your God, which he commanded you, and have gone and served other gods, and bowed yourselves to them; then shall the anger of the Lord be kindled against you, and ye shall perish quickly from off the good land which he hath given unto you" (Joshua 23:1-6).

The final chapters of this book may be grouped together since all the matters with which they deal are so closely linked. Joshua separated forty-eight cities from among the various tribes of Israel, and allotted them to the Levites; the warriors of two and a half tribes have returned to their homes which had already been given to them by Moses on the east side of the Jordan River. And the last chapters are full of the warnings of Joshua to his people not to forget the One True God Who had brought them into their possessions; who had fought for them; and who had kept His Word to them. He reminded the people that everything the Lord had promised to them had come true.

In his final speech, Joshua gathered all the tribes of Israel to Shechem, along with their leaders, elders, officers, and judges to present themselves before the Lord.

The speech was long and Joshua reminded them of their heritage, and that they must put away the strange gods from among them.

"Now therefore fear the Lord, and serve him in sincerity and in truth: and put away the gods which your fathers served on the other side of the flood, and in Egypt; and serve ye the Lord. And if it seem evil unto you to serve the Lord, choose you this day whom ye will serve; whether the gods which your fathers served that were on the other side of the flood, or the gods of the Amorites, in whose land ye dwell: but as for me and my house , we will serve the Lord" (Joshua 24:14-15).

It was on that day that Joshua made a covenant with the people, and wrote these words in the book of the law of God; he took up a big stone and set it under an oak, and called it a sanctuary of the Lord. It was to serve as a witness to the people that they had agreed with his words that day. After these words, Joshua, the servant of the Lord, died, and they buried him in Mount Ephraim, on the north side of the hill of Ga-ash.

Chapter 4

JUDGES

Using round figures for our dates, most of the events in the book of Judges occurred between 1400 and 1100 B.C. Unlike the book of Joshua, which recorded Israels victories, the book of Judges is the history of their defeat. They were destined to become a nation with a king, but not for two hundred years or more; this was a time in their history when they were learning to live together, and solve the problems of living closely with the Canaanite cities and the hostile nations on their borders. The reason they were constantly faced with these problems lay in the fact that they had wilfully disobeyed God's instructions to destroy the nations and tear down their altars. Consequently, the Israelites repeatedly fell into apostasy, followed by oppressions as the invading nations exploited them economically. The book of Judges received its name from the leaders who delivered Israel from a series of these foreign oppressions during that period of time between the death of Joshua, and the beginnings of the monarchy.

"And an an angel of the Lord came up from Gilgal to Bochim, and said, I made you to go up out of Egypt, and have brought you unto the land which I sware unto your fathers; and I said, I will never break my covenant with you. And ye shall make no league with the inhabitants of this land; ye shall throw down their altars: but ye have not obeyed my voice: why have ye done this? Wherefore I also said, I will not drive them out from before you; but they shall be as thorns in your sides, and their gods shall be a snare unto you" (Judges 2:1-3).

Religion Of Canaan

As stated previously, the most serious challenge to Israel's faith and survival, and one she was never able to overcome for long, was the religious practices of the Canaanites. The general Canaanite word for any divine being was *"el"*, but this was also the proper name of the main Canaanite god. He was thought of as a sky god who ruled over all the other gods. El's wife was Asherah. She was thought to be the mother goddess in charge of fertility. Asherah is mentioned in the Old Testament many times. In the King James Version of the Bible, her name is translated "grove," but in the more accurate translations, her proper name was given. She was usually represented by a tree or pole standing near an altar. The most important of the Canaanite gods, was an offspring of El and Asherah whose name was Baal. It was believed that he lived on the mountain tops in the north and controlled the rains and storms, and therefore the vegetation. In spite of the warnings and the commandmants of the Lord, the children of Israel compromised in their faith, and met with one disaster after the other. One other remark along this line which will help to shed some light on how easily this could happen is that the Israelites were scattered all over the countryside, intermingled with the pagan Canaanites, and separated from one another by valleys, ravines, rivers, mountains, and enemy-held territory which is cause for wonder how they held any unity and identity as God's covenant people.

When the angel of the Lord spoke to the children of Israel, they wept aloud, and named the place Bochim, and there they sacrificed to the Lord. The people served the Lord throughout the days of their leader , Joshua, and the elders that outlived him, who had seen the mighty miracles and wonders of the Lord; but as soon as that generation died there arose another generation who knew nothing about the Lord or His delivering power.

"And the children of Israel did evil in the sight of the Lord, and served Baalim: And they forsook the Lord God of their fathers, which brought brought them out of the land of Egypt, and followed other gods, of the gods of the people that were round about them, and bowed themselves unto them, and provoked the Lord to anger. And they forsook the Lord, and served Baal and Ashtaroth. And the anger of the Lord was hot against Israel, and he delivered them into the hands of spoilers that spoiled them, and he sold them into the hands of their enemies round about, so that they could not any

longer stand before their enemies. Withersoever they went out, the hand of the Lord was against them for evil, and the Lord had said, and as the Lord had sworn unto them: and they were greatly distressed" (Judges 2:11-15).

In the words of Matthew Henry, "The people of Israel forsook the God of Israel, and gave that worship and honour to the dunghill deities of the Canaanites which was due to him alone." The prophet Jeremiah cried, *"Hath a nation changed their gods, which are yet no gods? but my people have changed their glory for that which doth not profit. Be astonished, O ye heavens, at this, and be horribly afraid, be ye very desolate, saith the Lord. For my people have committed two evils; they have forsaken me the fountain of living waters, and hewed them out cisterns, broken cisterns, that can hold no water"* (2:11-13).

Nevertheless, the Lord raised up judges to deliver them from the hand of their enemies, but they would not listen, and kept bowing down to other gods. When God raised up a judge, He was with that judge to deliver His people. While the judge lived, they would walk in the ways of the Lord, but as soon as that judge died, they corrupted themselves again. They stubbornly returned to the evil customs of the wicked nations around them. For that very reason the Lord did not drive out those nations, and he would not allow the Israelites to drive them out; they were used to test the faith of His people. Nothing could be more evil than the evil they performed when they broke covenant with their God. One might say He offered them the flavor of wine; instead they chose the taste of ashes. They dwelt among the heathen nations, and married into their families.

Judges

Othni-el

The anger of the Lord was unleased upon His people, and He allowed King Cushanrishathaim of eastern Syria conquer them. For eight long years they were under his reign; but Israel cried out to God and He took pity on them and selected Caleb's nephew, Othni-el, to save them. He was led by the Spirit of the Lord, and he reformed and purged Israel, so that when he led the attack against King Cushanrishathaim, the Lord caused them to conquer him.

Ehud

For forty years during the reign of Othni-el, there was peace in the land, but he died, and Israel turned again to their sinful ways. God put it in the heart of King Eglon of Moab to conquer part of Israel at that time; the armies of the Ammonites and the Amalekites gladly linked forces with him against Israel, and the Israelies were defeated and the enemy took Jericho which is often called, *"the city of the palm trees."* For the next eighteen years the children of Israel paid heavy taxes to King Eglon.

"But when the children of Israel cried unto the Lord, the Lord raised them up a deliverer, Ehud the son of Gera, a Benjamite, a man lefthanded:[1] and by him the children of Israel sent a present unto Eglon the king of Moab" (Judges 3:15).

The time came to pay the annual tribute money to Eglon, and Ehud was selected to lead the delegation that

---

[1] In Judges 20:16, we note that the tribe of Benjamin seems to have had an unusual number of left-handed warriors; a curiosity of Bible History.

delivered it. He pretended that he had a secret message to deliver, and he managed to get an audience with the king. When they were alone, Ehud whipped out a small sword and assassinated the king by thrusting the deadly little weapon through his fat belly. Ehud then calmly locked the doors and left the palace. By the time the body was discovered, Ehud was well on his way back to the hill country of Ephraim. When he arrived, he blew the trumpet of victory, and told the children of God to follow him for the Lord had surely given them the victory. And for the next eighty years the land was in peace.

Shamgar

The next judge to rule over Israel was Shamgar, son of Anath. He had once killed hundreds of Philistines with an ox goad, and saved Israel from a disaster.

Deborah and Barak

Deborah and Barak were the fourth and fifth judges over Israel. Deborah is the only woman who is known to have been a judge. She was already known as a prophetess, and one to whom they could turn in times of trouble. When she saw the plight of the children of Israel, she called for Barak, a local military leader, and called for a showdown with Sisera, the commander of the Canaanite army. Barak agreed on the grounds that Deborah would go with him. But she told him that his dependence upon a woman would mean that a woman was going to receive the glory for the victory. This prophecy came true. Barak rounted the Canaanite army but allowed Sisera to escape. This is perhaps a somewhat familiar story to most. Sisera ran away on foot until he came ot the camp of Heber, the Kenite, who was on friendly terms with King Jabin of Hazor. Jael went out to meet Sisera and invited him into her tent. She assured him that he would be well protected. She gave him water to drink, and twice covered him with a blanket. He told her to stand by the tent door, and if anyone should ask for him to tell them he wasn't there.

Sisera fell into a dead sleep for he was worn from battle; she took a sharp tent peg and a hammer, and while he slept, she drove the peg through his temples and into the ground; and he died. When Barak came by looking for Sisera, Jael meet him and invited him in to see what she had done. From that time on, Israel became stronger and stronger against King Jabin until finally all his people were destroyed.

The Song Of Deborah

"Then sang Deborah and Barak the son of Abinoam on that day, saying, Praise ye the Lord for the avenging of Israel, when the people willingly offered themselves. Hear, O ye kings; give ear, O ye princes; I, even I, will sing unto the Lord; I will sing praise to the Lord God of Israel. Lord, when thou wentest out of Seir, when thou marchedst out of the field of Edom, the earth trembled, and the heavens dropped, the clouds also dropped water. The mountains melted from before the Lord, even that Sinai from before the Lord God of Israel. In the days of Shamgar the son of Anath, in the days of Jael, the highways were unoccupied, and the travellers walked through byways. The inhabitants of the villages ceased, they ceased in Israel, until that I Debokrah

arose, that I arose a mother in Israel. They chose new gods; then was war in the gates: was there a shield or spear seen among forty thousand in Israel? My heart is toward the governors of Israel, that offered themselves willingly wmong the people. Bless ye the Lord...Awake, awake, Deborah: awake, awake, utter a song: arise, Barak, and lead thy captivity captive, thou son of Abinoam" (Judges 5:1-12).

And the land had rest for forty years. This particular victory had given the people ample reason for praising God. They had become few in number yet God continued to deliver them and give them dominion over the evil nations.

Gideon

"And the children of Israel did evil in the sight of the Lord: and the Lord delivered them into the hand of Midian seven years. And the hand of Midian prevailed against Israel: and because of the Midianites the children of Israel made them the dens which are in the mountains, and caves, and strong holds" (Judges 6:1-2).

We have here Israel's sin renewed, and they did evil in the sight of the Lord. Here we quote from Matthew Henry, *"The burnt child dreads the fire; yet this perverse unthinking people, that had so often smarted sorely for their idolatry, upon a little respite of God's judgments return to it again. This people hath a revolting rebellious heart, not kept in awe by the terror of God's judgments, nor engaged in honour and gratitude by the great things he had done for them to keep themselves in his love. The providence of God will not change the hearts and lives of sinners.''*

The Midianites were so cruel that the Israelites retreated to the mountains, living in caves and dens. When they planted their crops, the evil Midianites and other neighboring natins destroyed their crops. They plundered the countryside as far away as Gaza, leaving nothing to eat, and taking the animals with them. Israel was reduced to abject poverty, and they cried out to God for help.

"And it came to pass, when the children of Israel cried unto the Lord because of the Midianites, That the Lord sent a prophet unto the children of Israel, which said unto them, Thus saith the Lord God of Israel, I brought you up from Egypt, and brought you forth out of the house of bondage; And I delivered you out of the hand of the Egyptians, and out of the hand of all that oppressed you, and drave them out from before you, and gave you this land; And I said unto you, I am the Lord your God; fear not the gods of the Amorites, in whose land ye dwell: but ye have not obeyed my voice" (Judges 6:7-10).

Before the Lord God sent an angel to raise them up a Saviour, he sent a prophet to reprove them for sin, and to bring them to repentance. He is not named, but he sounds out a strong warning to the children of Israel which they need to hear.

The calling of Gideon ushers in the second period in the history of the judges. It lasted less than a century, and things were rapidly hastening towards the final crisis. One day while Gideon, Joash's son, was threshing wheat in the bottom of a grape press (a pit where grapes were pressed to make wine), the angel of the Lord appeared to him. Gideon was hiding his work from the Midianites.

"And the angel of the Lord appeared unto him, and said unto him, The Lord is with thee, thou mighty man of valour. And Gideon said unto him, Oh my Lord, if the Lord be with us, why then is all this befallen us? and where be all his miracles which our fathers told us of, saying, Did not the Lord bring us up from Egypt? but now the Lord hath forsaken us, and delivered us into the hands of the Midianites" (Judges 6:12-13). In many ways this particular period of Israel's history was the worst she had ever suffered. Gideon's heart was heavy as he watched the demise of Israel. The Midianites and their camels conquered and covered the land like hoards of grasshoppers; the results was devastating. But God heard the cry of his people, and sent an angel to converse with this mighty man of valor.

When the angel declared that the Lord stood by the Israelites, Gideon questioned the validity of such a statement in view of the obvious condition of both the land and its people. He made the same declaration that most Christians make when reminded of the promises of God in the midst of a fiery trial. Where is the God of yesterday? We do not see His miracles? How is it we have fallen so low? And when the Lord told him he would deliver the people, this seemed to be the height of the ridiculous.

Gideon asked for a sign from the Lord to prove he was not imagining things even though the Lord had just told him to go, and He would be with him. Gideon asked his guest to linger until he could go get a present for him. He prepared food, and set it before the Angel. The Angel of the Lord told him to place the meat and bread upon a rock, then pour the broth over it. Gideon did as the Angel requested; the Angel touched the meat and bread with his staff; fire flamed up from the rock and consumed the meat and bread; then the Angel disappeared.

Jehovah-shalom

"And when Gideon perceived that he was an angel of the Lord, Gideon said, Alas, O Lord God! for because I have seen an angel of the Lord face to face. And the Lord said unto him, Peace be unto thee; fear not: thou shalt not die. Then Gideon built an altar there unto the Lord, and called it Jehovah-shalom: unto this day it is yet in Ophrah of the Abi-ezrites" (Judges 6:22- 24).

The Holy War

Gideon had now purified himself and his house, and was ready to serve the Lord. His first task was a most difficult one. Gideon was told to tear down the idolatrous altars his father had erected and to build an altar to Yahweh on the same spot. Obediently, he did as he was told. He knew there would be trouble from the townspeople who had evidently become ardent devotees of Baal. He was actually taking his life into his own hand, and must lean totally upon the promises he had received from the Lord Himself. His worst fears were justified; the next morning when it was discovered that someone had torn down the altar of Baal, they sought out Gideon. But Gideon's father talked them out ot it. He reasoned that Baal needed no help avenging his opponent if he were truly a god.

Gideon's Fleece

"And Gideon said unto God, If thou wilt save Israel by mine hand, as thou hast said, Behold, I will put a fleece of wool in the floor; and if the dew be on the fleece only, and it be dry upon all the earth beside, then shall I know that thou wilt save Israel by mine hand, as thou hast said. And it was so: for he rose up early on the morrow, and thrust the fleece together, and wringed the dew out of the fleece, a bowl full of water. And Gideon said unto God, Let not thine anger be hot against me, and I will speak but this once: let me prove, I pray thee, but this once with the fleece; let it now be dry only upon the fleece, and upon all the ground let there be dew. And God did so that night for it was dry upon the fleece only, and there was dew on all the ground" (Judges 6:37-40).

Now God was ready to perform a miracle of such dynamic proportions that all of Israel would know that He was their God. He had chosen Gideon as their leader. Gideon prepared the army to attack the Midianites, but the army was too large. If that many men went to fight, the Israelites could claim credit for winning the battle. God ordered that all the men who were afraid should go home. This seemed strange to the men, but of the 32,000, 22,000 went back home. This left Gideon with a small army of 10,000 to fight against the Midianites. The Lord spoke again and told Gideon he still had too many men.

"And the Lord said unto Gideon, The people are yet too many; bring them down unto the water, and I will try them for thee there: and it shall be, that of whom I say unto thee, This shall go with thee, the same shall go with thee; and of whomsoever I say unto thee, This shall not go with thee, the same shall not go" (Judges 7:4).

Gideon took the men to the water to drink. God told him to divide them into two groups and decide who would fight by the way they drank from the brook. The men who lapped the water like a dog laps were chosen, and the others sent home. This left Gideon with 300 fighting men. Certainly they looked like a small group camped on a hill above the large camp of the Midianites. During the night Gideon and his servant crept down close to the enemy camp and listened as two of the soldiers talked. One man had dreamed a strange dream; the other soldier told him it was a dream of how God would deliver them into the hands of the Israelites. The encouraged Gideon so he slipped back into his camp and made ready to attack. He divided the men into three groups, each having one hundred men. Then he gave each man a trumpet, pitcher, and a torch. He told the men to light the torches and then cover them with the pitchers. In the night the three companies crept down the mountainside to the Midianite camp, and took their positions on three sides - then Gideon blew loudly upon his horn, hit his pitcher against a stone and broke it, causing his torch to shine through the darkness, and all the 300 men did the same. Then they shouted: *"The sword of the Lord and of Gideon" (Judges 7:18)!*

When the Midianites heard the noise of the trumpets and all the shouting, they were seized with fear, and fled in utter confusion, fighting and killing one another. And the land had forty years of rest under the leadership of Gideon. Then Gideon died and the children of Israel turned again and worshipped idols.

Six Judges

Tola was the seventh judge for twenty-three years. Jair was their eighth judge for twenty-two years. With the death of each judge, the children of Israel did evil in the sight of the Lord. Then the Lord sold them into the hands of the Philistines, and into the hands of the children of the Amorites; then God raised up the ninth judge, Jephthah. And the Lord gave him victory over their enemies. Zephthah died and the children of Israel did evil in the sight of the Lord and went after other gods. The Lord delivered them into the hands of the Philistines for forty years. The tenth judge over Israel was Ibzan who ruled for seven years; he died and Elon became the eleventh judge; he ruled for ten years over Israel. Abdon was the twelfth judge; he ruled for eight years, then he died.

Samson

The children of Israel did evil again in the sight of the Lord; and the Lord delivered them into the hands of the Philistines to serve them for forty years. They were non- semitic people, and often called *"the uncircumcised."* They settled in the plain and low hill country of southwestern Palestine, and were a part of the great invasion of the sea peoples referred to by Rameses III of Egypt about 1200 B.C. They were the leading enemy of Israel from the time of Samson to the middle of King David's reign.

Samson was Israels thirteenth judge, and his story a very uncommon one. He was from the tribe of Dan. Dan signifies a judge or judgment. Probably Jacob foretold of the birth of Samson when he said that Dan would judge his people. In other words, he would produce a judge for the people. His parents had been childless for a long time. Then the angel of the Lord brought the *"good news"* to

Manoah's wife that a child was to be born to them, and he would be a Nazarite from the womb to the day of his death; and no razor was to touch his head.

"And the woman bare a son, and called his name Samson: and the child grew, and the Lord blessed him. And the spirit of the Lord began to move him at times in the camp of Dan between Zorah and Eshtaol" (Judges 13:24-25).

Samson married a Philistine woman from the town of Timnath; on his way to tend to the marriage plans, Samson wandered off from his parents, and a lion leaped out at him, ready to attack, but Samson caught the lion and killed him with his bare hands. God had given Samson supernatural strength for a special purpose. Once he killed a thousand Philistines with just the jaw bone of a donkey. *"And it came ot pass afterward, that he loved a woman in the valley of Sorek, whose name was Delilah"* (Judges 16:4).

For the second time Samson fell in love with a Philistine woman. By this time the Philistine leaders were plotting his death. They came to Delilah with a bargain. They would give her eleven hundred pieces of silver for the secret behind Samson's strength. Finally, Samson confided in her that he was a Nazarite, and if he shaved his hair his strength would be gone. When he fell asleep, she slipped into the room and cut his hair; Samson woke to find that the Lord had left him helpless. When he faced the Philistines, they put out his eyes and brought him down to Gaza and bound him, and he was placed in their prison. The people rejoiced and worshiped Dagon for delivering Samson into their hands.

"And Samson called called unto the Lord, and said, O Lord God, remember me, I pray thee, and strengthen me, I pray thee, only this once, O God that I may be at once avenged of the Philistines for two eyes. And Samson took hold of the two middle pillars upon which the house stood, and on which it was borne up, of the one with his right hand, and of the other with his left. And Samson said, Let me die with the Philistines. And he bowed himself with all his might; and the house fell upon the lords, and upon all the people that were therein. So the dead which he slew at his death were more than they which he slew in his life" (Judges 16:28-30).

Sampson judged Israel for twenty years.

Chapter 5

RUTH

The book of Ruth is usually entitled *"A Love Story."* It took place during the first half of the reign of the judges. Ruth is a type of the church: the *"gentile bride of Christ."* Boaz speaks to us of Christ our Kinsman Redeemer.

Famine in Judah

"Now it came to pass in the days when the judges ruled, that there was a famine in the land. And a certain man of Bethlehem-judah went to sojourn in the country of Moab, he, and his wife, and his two sons" (Ruth 1:1).

Ruth was a gentile who married into a Jewish family and thereby came into the line of David, and through it all Gentiles have been blessed. This little love story sandwiched in between the Judges and the books of Samuel tends to give the reader some moments of respite from wars and oppressions and more wars. The name Ruth means, *"a friend."*

This story began at Bethlehem (house of Bread), and the first name mentioned is Elimelech (My God is King), and Israelite, his wife, Naomi (pleasantness or favour), and two sons, Mahlon (joy, or song), and Chilion (ornament, or perfectness).

During famine they left the *"House of Bread"* and traveled to a strange land in search of *"succour"* in Moab. Elimelech (my God is my King) died; the two sons took wives of the Moabites, Orpah, and Ruth, then died leaving Naomi destitute. By her own testimony she changed from Naomi (pleasantness, sweetness, favour, to Mara (bitterness). In that strange land *"My God is King,"* died; so do *"Song and Perfectness."* After ten bitter years Naomi returned to the *"House of Bread."* We see in all this a striking type of Israel. Naomi, the pathetic remnant returned to her place of beginnings empty and seeking the Lord for she had heard He had visited her land giving the people bread.

Under heavy testing, Israel denounced God and went astray over and over until she became like a putrefying sore in the eyes of her King. Israel was Elimelech, and could say, *"My God is King,"* and he (Israel) was married to Naomi (pleasantness, favour, and blessing); born to this union was *"Song and Perfectness."* But when Elimelech died, no longer could Israel say, *"My God is King."* The Song, the Blessings and the Favour died with him. (This stands as only one of the many illustrations drawn from this little book). One strong point to be made is that to be out of the will of the Lord is to backslide.

We have three women who have been deprived of their husbands. They stand at the *"cross-roads"* of their lives. Naomi insisted that both her daughters-in-law return to their respective families. Tearfully, Orpha kissed her and left, but Ruth refused to leave.

"And Ruth said, Entreat me not to leave thee, or to return from following after thee: for whiter thou goest, I will go; and where thou lodgest, I will lodge: thy people shall be my people, and thy God my God: Where thou diest, will I die, and there will I be buried: the Lord do so to me, and more also, if aught but death part thee and me" (Ruth 1:16-17).

So Naomi and Ruth returned to Bethlehem in the beginning of the barley harvest, and Ruth immediately went into the fields to gather grain with the other reapers. It was a custom in Israel for the reapers to leave some of the grain for the poor people to gather, and this was what Ruth gathered as she followed them. It was in the field of Boaz that she gleaned; Boaz was Naomi's wealthy kinsman by marriage.

"And, behold, Boaz came from Bethlehem, and said unto the reapers, The Lord be with you. And they answered him, The Lord bless thee. Then said Boaz unto his servant who was set over the reapers, Whose damsel is this? And the servant who was set over the reapers answered and said, It is the Moabitish damsel who came back with Naomi out of the country of Moab. And she said, I pray you, let me glean and gather after the reap-

ers among the sheaves. So she came, and hath continued even from the morning until now, except that she tarried a little in the house. Then said Boaz unto Ruth, Hearest thou not, my daughter? Go not to glean in another field, neither go from hence, but abide here fast by my maidens: Let thine eyes be on the field that they do reap, and go thou after them: have I not charged the young men that they shall not touch thee? and when thou art athirst, go unto the vessels, and drink of that which the young men have drawn. The she fell on her face, and bowed herself to the ground, and said unto him, Why have I found grace in thine eyes, that thou shouldest take knowledge of me, seeing I am a stranger? And Boaz answered and said unto her, It hath fully been shown me, all that thou hast done for thy mother-in-law since the death of thine husband, and how thou hast left thy father and thy mother, and the land of thy nativity, and art come unto a people whom thou knewest not heretofore. The Lord recompense thy work, and a full reward be given thee by the Lord God of Israel, under whose wings thou art come to trust. Then she said, Let me find favor in thy sight, my lord; for thou hast comforted me, and because thou hast spoken friendly unto thine handmaid, though I be not like unto one of thine handmaidens. And Boaz said unto her, At mealtime come thou hither, and eat of the bread, and dip thy morsel in the vinegar. And she sat beside the reapers; and he reached her parched corn, and she did eat, and was sufficed, and left. And when she was risen up to glean, Boaz commanded his young men, saying, Let her glean even among the sheaves, and reproach her not: And let fall also some of the handfuls of purpose for her, and leave them, that she may glean them, and rebuke her not" (Ruth 2:4-16).[1]

Ruth rushed home at the end of the day to tell Naomi of her new blessing, and what unexpected kindness she had experienced at the hand of Boaz; Naomi was delighted that they had found such favour , and she told Ruth that he was their nearest kinsmen. Naomi had the wheels of her mind turning in the direction of a husband for Ruth, and Boaz was the perfect choice. He had been kind to them, and he was, after all, a close relative.

Naomi instructed Ruth in the proper thing for her to do. She went down to the threshing floor, and waited until Boaz retired and slept. Then she lifted the covers and slipped quietly beneath them and lay at his feet. At midnight he turned over and sat up with a start to find Ruth lying at his feet.

"And he said, Who art thou? And she answered, I am Ruth thine handmaid: spread therefore thy skirt over thine handmaid; for thou art a near kinsman. And he said, Blessed be thou of the Lord, my daughter: for thou hast shown more kindness in the latter end than at the beginning, inasmuch as thou followedst not young men, whether poor or rich. And now, my daughter, fear not; for I will do to thee all that thou requirest: for the city of my people doth know that thou art a virtuous woman. And now it is true that I am thy near kinsman: howbeit there is a kinsman nearer than I" (Ruth 3:9-12).

---

[1] Salmon was the father of Boaz (Rahab was his mother). Boaz was the father of Obed, (Ruth was his mother). Obed was the father of Jesse, and Jesse was the father of King David.

Boaz blessed the Lord for a woman like Ruth; he recognized that there was a difference in their ages, but he complimented her that she was even kinder to Naomi now than ever before as she had put aside all her personal feelings to marry and give Naomi an heir. He called her *"my daughter,"* and told her not to worry that he would tend to all the marriage plans. Apparently, he had checked into this situation for he told Ruth that she had a relative who was more closely related to her than he, but he would talk with him come the morning light.

"So Boaz took Ruth, and she was his wife: and when he went in unto her, the Lord gave her conception, and she bare a son. And the women said unto Naomi, Blessed be the Lord, which hath not left thee this day without a kinsman, that his name may be famous in Israel" (Ruth 4:13-14).

Chapter 6

THE REIGN OF SAMUEL

First and Second Samuel are counted as one book in the Hebrew Bible. In this first section of Samuel we are introduced to Hannah, a woman who knew the importance of keeping her vows unto the Lord. After a long silence in the story, interest turns once again to the sacred Tabernacle which God had pitched among men so long ago, and the Priesthood which He had instituted. The period of the Judges had run its full course, and still Israel was not saved. From the birth of Samuel to the death of Solomon was termed the United Hebrew Monarchy. During this period of Israel's history, she rose to new heights of material splendor and national fame. One writer stated that the period of the Judges was fraught with danger and uncertainty, and the fate of Israel hung frequently in the balance. There were times when it was questionable whether the tribes would survive or go under; whether they would retain their unique identity or melt into the crowds and be forgotten as the chosen of God and forget their covenant and adopt the gods of the land. But with the birth of Samuel, the nation of Israel experienced some *"new beginnings"* in not only her religious commitments but also economically.

While the judges ruled Israel, the house of worship stood at Shiloh, near the center of the land. The Israelites were commanded to come to Shiloh *"yearly"* to offer sacrifices on the altar that stood before the tabernacle, the tent of worship that Moses and the people had made in the wilderness.

Elkanah (God-acquired), a man from the tribe of Ephraim, who lived in Ramathaim-zophim, in the hills of Ephraim, had two wives, Peninnah (pearl or coral), and Hannah (favor-grace), but Hannah had no children which might account for the double marriage.

Hannah's Prayer and Vow

"So Hannah rose up after they had eaten in Shiloh, and after they had drunk. Now Eli the priest sat upon a seat by a post of the temple of the Lord. And she was in bitterness of soul, and prayed unto the Lord, and wept sore. And she vowed a vow, and said, O Lord of hosts, if thou wilt indeed look on the affliction of thine handmaid, and remember me, and not forget thine handmaid, but wilt give unto thine handmaid a man child, then I will give him unto the Lord all the days of his life, and there shall no razor come upon his head. And it came to pass, as she continued praying before the Lord,

that Eli marked her mouth. Now Hanaah, she spake in her heart; only her lips moved, but her voice was not heard: therefore Eli thought she had been drunken. And Eli said unto her, How long wilt thou be drunken? put away thy wine from thee. And Hannah answered and said, No, my lord, I am a woman of a sorrowful spirit: I have drunk neither wine nor strong drink, but have poured out my soul before the Lord. Count not thine handmaid for a daughter of Belial: for out of the abundance of my complaint and grief have I spoken hitherto. Then Eli answered and said, Go in peace: and the God of Israel grant thee thy petition that thou hast asked of him" (I Samuel 1:9-17).

Every year at that time, Elkanah celebrated the happy occasion by giving presents to Peninnah and her children; but Hannah had no children, so her husband gave her one gift. Peninnah taunted Hannah because of her barrenness which did not help the situation.

Hannah's grief was much deeper than her husband understood. She would not eat, and during this feastive time, she sat and wept before the Lord. One evening she went to the Tabernacle and Eli, the old priest, was sitting at his usual place beside the door. Hannah prayed and groaned from deep within. Her grief was so great she couldn't utter a sound. Eli accused her of being drunk because her lips moved, but he heard not a sound.

Hannah vowed a vow unto the Lord. If He would be merciful and give her a son, she would wean him, and dedicate him back to God. She promised that her son would be wholly dedicated to the work of the Lord from birth. She made a vow to God that was to last for a lifetime.

Before the time came for another Passover, Hannah had the child of her prayers whom she named Samuel (Heard of God). She did not go to Shiloh until the third year, when the child was fully weaned; then she presented herself once more before Eli.

"And when she had weaned him, she took him up with her, with three bullocks, and one ephah of flour, and a bottle of wine, and brought him unto the house of the Lord in Shiloh: and the child was young. And they slew the bullock, and brought the child to Eli. And she said, Oh my lord, as thy soul liveth, my lord, I am the woman that stood by thee here, praying unto the Lord. For this child I prayed; and the Lord hath given me my petition which I asked of him: Therefore also I have lent him to the Lord; as long as he liveth he shall be lent to the Lord. And he worshipped the Lord there" (I Samuel 1:24-28).

Hannah had entered into her own personal covenant with the Lord. She was a godly woman and knew the penalty for vowing unto Him and forgetting that vow. The burnt offering which they offered upon the altar was for the dedication of this child. It was a thanksgiving offering to Him. She did not use the word *"lent"* in the sense that we do as we loan and take back. She used *"Shaol"* and it was repeated by her. Samuel was not only asked of God, but also lent to God. What we give to God is what we have first received from Him. All our gifts to Him were once His gifts to us. In I Chronicles 29:14,16, we read, *"But who am I, and what is my people, that we should be able to offer so willingly after this sort? for all things come of thee, and of thine own have we given thee... O Lord* our God, all this store that we have prepared to build ee an house for thine holy name cometh of thine hand, and is all thine own."

Hannah's Song

"And Hannah prayed, and said, My heart rejoiceth in the Lord, mine horn is exalted in the Lord: my mouth is enlarged over mine enemies; because I rejoice in thy salvation.

There is none holy as the Lord: for there is none beside thee: neither is there any rock like our God, He will keep the feet of the saints, and the wicked shall be silent in darkness; for by strength shall no man prevail. The adversaries of the Lord shall be broken to pieces; out of heaven shall he thunder upon them: the Lord shall judge the ends of the earth; and he shall give strength unto his king, and exalt the horn of his anointed" (I Samuel 1,2,9,10).

In Luke 1:46-55, Mary echoes these words in the *Magnificat*. Hannah left Samuel with Eli and went back to Ramah with her husband. The child ministered unto the Lord before Eli the priest.

"But Samuel ministered before the Lord, being a child, girded with a linen ephod. Moreover his mother made him a little coat, and brought it to him from year to year, when she came up with her husband to offer the yearly sacrifice...And the child Samuel grew, and was in favour both with the Lord, and also with men" (I Samuel 2:18,26).

Hophni And Phinehas

These were the two sons of Eli who were evil and did not respect the things of God. The sin of these young men was very great in the eyes of the Lord for they treated with contempt the offerings brought by the people to the altar. Eli was old but he knew what was happening with his sons. He knew they were seducing the young women who assisted at the entrance of the Tabernacle. Eli tried to counsel with his sons, but they refused to listen to him.

"And there came a man of God unto Eli, and said unto him, Thus saith the Lord, Did I plainly appear unto the house of thy father, when they were in Egypt in Pharaoh's house? And did I choose him out of all the tribes of Israel to be my priest, to offer upon mine altar, to burn incense, to wear an ephod before me? and did I give unto the house of thy father all the offerings made by fire of the children of Israel? Wherefore kick ye at my sacrifice and at mine offering, which I have commanded in my habitation; and honourest thy sons above me, to make yourselves fat with the chieftest of all the offerings of Israel my people? Wherefore the Lord God of Israel saith, I said indeed that thy house, and the house of thy father, should walk before me for ever: but now the Lord saith, Be it far from me; for them that honour me I will honour, and they that despise me shall be lightly esteemed. Behold, the days come, that I will cut off thine arm, and the arm of thy father's house, that there shall not be an old man in thine house. And thou shalt see an enemy in my habitation, in all the wealth which God shall give Israel: and there shall not be an old man in thine house for ever. And the man of thine,

whom I shall not cut off from mine altar, shall be to consume thine eyes, and to grieve thine heart: and all the increase of thine house shall die in the flower of their age. And this shall be a sign unto thee, that shall come upon thy two sons, on Hophni and Phinehas; in one day they shall die both of them. And I will raise me up a faithful priest, that shall do according to that which is in mine heart and in my mind: and I will build him a sure house; and he shall walk before mine anointed for ever. And it shall come to pass, that every one that is left in thine house shall come and crouch to him for a piece of silver and a morsel of bread, and shall say, Put me, I pray thee, into one of the priests' offices, that I may eat a piece of bread" (I Samuel 2:27-36).

God told Eli that he and his family would see bad days because they had misused the people who brought sacrifices to the tabernacle; He said they had taken from the people and heaped it upon themselves and grown fat and lazy, and none of them would live to be old.

Samuel Called

"And the child Samuel ministered unto the Lord before Eli. And the word of the Lord was precious in those days; there was no open vision. And it came to pass at that time, when Eli was laid down in his place, and his eyes began to wax dim, that he could not see; And ere the lamp of God went out in the temple of the Lord, where the ark of God was, and Samuel was laid down to sleep; That the Lord called Samuel: and he answered, Here am I" (I Samuel 3:1-4).

Young Samuel jumped to his feet; he thought the old priest had called out for him. Eli had not called, so he went back to his bed. God called again; again Samuel jumped up and ran to Eli and asked what he wanted. Again he told him he had not called to him, so Samuel headed back for his bed. The Lord called out to him the third time, and for the third time Samuel ran to Eli inquiring of him his need. On the third try, Eli realized it was the Lord calling to the young man. He told the child to go back and lie down for it was the Lord calling him. He should make his response to the Lord. Samuel said, *"Speak Lord, I am listening."*

"And the Lord said to Samuel, Behold, I will do a thing in Israel, at which both the ears of every one that heareth it shall tingle. In that day I will perform against Eli all things which I have spoken concerning his house: when I begin, I will also make an end" (I Samuel 3:11-13).

It was a shocking thing the Lord was pronouncing that He would do in Israel because of the sins of Eli and his sons. This was the message that young Samuel was told to tell the old priest. Somewhat reluctantly, due to the age difference, Samuel delivered the entire message the next day; old Eli received it as from the Lord, and said the Lord should do what was right, and what seemed to be good in His own eyes.

Samuel grew and the Lord guided him, and people listened to his counsel for they knew he was a prophet called of God. The Lord gave many messages to Samuel there at Shiloh, which he delivered to the people.

It is at this point in Israel's history that we may view their transition from Theocracy to the Monarch; in other words, at this point there is a slow transition from judges to kings over the people. God had already informed Eli that desolation was to come to his house. It is believed that Samuel was about twelve when the Lord spoke to him; twenty years have passed and nothing had changed in Shiloh regarding the old priest and his family except he had grown fatter and was blind from age.

The Ark Of God Captured

After the Philistines advanced towards ancient Jebus, killing four thousand Israelites, the Hebrews questioned why God had struck such a deadly blow at His people. So they decided to move the Ark from Shiloh to their camp and use it against the invading Philistines. Since the Ark had preceded them at the crossing of Jordan and at the battle of Jericho, they reasoned within themselves this was the answer. When the children of Israel saw the Ark coming, they shouted with joy; their shouts were so loud they reached the ears of the Philistines who panicked when they heard the Ark had arrived in the enemies camp. The Philistines had heard how God always fought for His children. The Philistine leaders said they must fight as they had never fought before or they would become slaves to Israel.

The Philistines fought a fierce battle and succeeded in killing 30,000 Hebrew soldiers, and they captured the Ark. The wicked sons of Eli were killed in battle. A man from the tribe of Benjamin left his ranks and ran into Shiloh; he rent his clothes and threw earth upon his head. He told Eli the bad news: *"Israel is fled! There has been a mighty slaughter! Your two sons are slain! And the Ark of God has been taken!"*

I-chabod

When the old priest heard all that had come to pass, he fell backward off his seat and broke his neck; he died at the gate of the temple after having judged Israel for forty years. When Phinehas's wife heard that her husband was dead; her father-in-law was dead; and the Ark had been taken, she labored and brought forth a child and named him I-chabod, *"The Glory has departed from Israel."*

The Philistine took the Ark from Eben-ezer to Ashdod. They set it in the house of Dagon beside Dagon. The next morning morning Dagon had fallen on his face before the Ark of the Lord. They set him up but it happen again - the idol fell flat on its face; this time its head and hands had been cut off and were found lying in the doorway.

Return of the Ark

The Lord began to destroy the people of Ashdod and of nearby villages with plagues and boils. The people cried out that the Ark had to be sent back to God's people before they were all killed. The leaders of their cities decided it should be taken to Gath. When the Ark arrived at Gath, the Lord began destorying the people; they were all filled with fear and sent the Ark on Ekron; but when the people of Ekron saw the Ark coming, they ran wild and cried, *"They are bringing the Ark of the Lord God here to kill us!* The Ark of the Lord remained in the Philistine country for seven months then the city official met to decide its fate. They questioned among themselves what kind of guilt offering should go with the Ark. (In all religions offerings are a part of the worship). It was to be sent back on a new cart; likewise, the Lord Jesus rode on an ass where on never man sat (Mark 11:2). His body was placed in Joseph's new tomb.

"And they laid the ark of the Lord upon the cart, and the coffer with the mice of gold and the images of their emerods. And the kine took the straight way to the way of Beth-shemesh, and went along the highway, lowing as they went, and turned not aside to the right hand or to the left; the lords of the Philistines went after them unto the border of Beth-shemkesh" (ISamuel 6:11- 12).

For twenty years the Ark of the Lord abode in Kirjath-jearim. During those years Israel wept for it seemed that the Lord had totally abandoned them. Samuel called them together an announced if they would put away their strange gods, and get serious about serving the Lord God, the Lord would turn from His anger and rescue them. So they gathered together and drew water from a well and poured it out before the Lord. They fasted all that day as a sign to the Lord of their sorrow. It was at Mizpah that Samuel became Israel's judge. In their next battle against the Philistines, the Lord fought for them, and they subdued their enemies.

Chapter 7

THE REIGN OF SAUL

"So the Philistines were subdued, and they came no more into the coast of Israel: and the hand of the Lord was against the Philistines all the days of Samuel. And the cities which the Philistines had taken from Israel were restored to Israel, from Ekron even unto Gath; and the coasts thereof did Israel deliver out of the hands of the Philistines. And there was peace between Israel and the Amorites. And Samuel judged Israel all the days of his life. And he went from year to year in circuit to Bethel, and Gilgal, and Mizpeh, and judged Israel in all those places. And his return was to Ramah; for there was his house; and there he judged Israel; and there he built an altar unto the Lord" (I Samuel 7:13-17).

So Samuel continued to judge Israel all the days of his life; he served as a circuit judge, traveling from city to city. He judged over both the political and religious matters of his people. He also established schools of the prophets in those posts. These schools, no doubt, were largely responsible for the improved conditions that were to come in the political, moral and religious life of Israel. But Samuel grew old and the people demanded a king to rule over them.

"And said unto him, Behold, thou art old, and thy sons walk not in thy ways: now make us a king to judge us like all the nations" (I Samuel 8:5).

Samuel's sons did not walk in the ways of the Lord; they took bribes and turned aside after money and perverted judgment, so the people gathered before Samuel and demanded a king to rule over them like the other nations. This suggestion was very displeasing to Samuel. He saw at once the danger of forsaking the One True God to rule over the people. However, he faithfully took the matter up with the Lord.

Israel Rejected God

"And the Lord said unto Samuel, Hearken unto the voice of the people in all that they say unto thee: for they have not rejected thee, but they have rejected me, that I should not reign over them. According to all the works which they have done since the day that I brought them up out of Egypt even unto this day, wherewith they have forsaken me, and served other gods, so do they also unto thee. Now therefore hearken unto their voice: howbeit yet protest solemnly unto them, and show them the manner of the king that shall reign over them" (I Samuel 8:7-9)

Samuel gathered the people before him and told them the warnings of the Lord. He warned them what manner of king would rule over them: (1) he will take your sons, and appoint them for himself; (2) he will make them run before his chariots; some will be made to lead his troops into battle; (3) some will be slaves and be forced to plow the fields and harvest his crops; (4) some will make his war-weapons and chariot equipment; (5) your daughters will be taken from you and forced to cook,bake, and make his perfumes; (6) he will steal your fields, and vineyards and olive groves; (7) he will take a tenth of your harvest and give it to his friends; (8) He will take your slaves from you, your young men, and use your animals for his own personal gain; (9) he will take a tenth of your flocks, and you will be his slaves.

Samuel surely must have wept as he told the people how their demand for a king would cause them to weep bitterly before the Lord one day, but He would not listen to them. But the people refused to listen to either God or Samuel. They repeated the fact that they wanted to be like other nations.

Saul Anointed

Saul (the asked for) was a striking figure possessing several admirable qualities. He was a man of large physique and quite handsome; there was none like him among all the people. When he first came on the scene, he was modest and humble. He had not sought the kingly office, and apparently was not too eager to serve. At least Saul had a good beginning. He had been given the honor of being Israel's first king; and he was all but unanimously accepted into office.

Kish, Saul's father, sent his son and a servant out to seek the donkeys that had strayed from home. After three days, and many miles of travel, Saul told the servant it might be best to head back home lest his father begin to worry over him instead of the lost animals. We learn from this part of the narrative how God works on both ends of the line. Saul's servant suggested that they were close to the home of the "seer" who might know the location of their donkeys.

"Now the Lord had told Samuel in his ear a day before Saul came, saying, Tomorrow about this time I will send thee a man out of the land of Benjamin, and thou shalt anoint him to be captain over my people out of the hand of the Philistines: for I have looked upon my people, because their cry is come unto me. And when Samuel saw Saul, the Lord said unto him, Behold the man whom I spake to thee of! this same shall reign over my people" (I Samuel 9:15-17).

Samuel told Saul the donkeys that strayed away three days before were found, and that he should not worry for all of Israel was his. Saul reminded Samuel that he was from the tribe of Benjamin, the smallest in Israel, and his family was the least important of all the families of the tribes - surely he had the wrong man.

Samuel took Saul and his servant into the great hall and they ate at the head table along with thirty guest who had been invited the day the Lord told Samuel the *"king was coming."* Next, Samuel accompanied the servant and Saul to the edge of the city where the servant was sent on ahead. It was then Samuel told Saul that the Lord had selected him to be the king of Israel. He took a flask of oil and poured it over the head of Saul, and kissed him and said that he was following the instructions of the Lord.

"After that thou shalt come to the hill of God, where is the garrison of the Philistines: and it shall come to pass, when thou art come thither to the city, that thou shalt meet a company of prophets coming down from the high place with a psaltery, and a tabret, and a pipe, and a harp, before them; and they shall prophesy: And the spirit of the Lord will come upon thee, and thou shalt prophesy with them, and shalt be turned into another man...for God is with thee" (I Samuel 10:5-7).

Kingdom Established

Saul proved himself courageous even before he took over the duties as king of Israel. Nahash the Ammonite came against the city of Jabesh-gilead. The citizens of the city were not fighters and asked for peace, offering to become servants. Nahash agreed on the condition that he could gouge out the right eye of every one to serve as a disgrace upon all Israel. They asked for seven days to seek help, and if no help came, they would agree to his terms. Saul heard of the plot and the Spirit of the Lord came upon him and he became very angry. He cut two oxen into pieces and sent them throughout all Israel with the news that anyone refusing to follow Samuel and Saul into battle would have their oxen cut in the same manner. All the people followed him and they saved the city. At Gilgal, Samuel held a solemn ceremony before the Lord, and they crowned Saul their king, and all the people rejoiced greatly.

After Samuel addressed the people, and rehearsed in their ears once again their responsibility towards God, he invited them to stand still and see once again what the Lord would do for His people right before their eyes.

"Now therefore stand and see this great thing, which the Lord will do before your eyes. Is it not wheat harvest today? I will call unto the Lord, and he shall send thunder and rain; that ye may perceive and see that your wickedness is great, which ye have done in the sight of the Lord, in asking you a king. So Samuel called unto the Lord; and the Lord sent thunder and rain that day: and all the people greatly feared the Lord and Samuel. And all the people said unto Samuel, Pray for thy servants unto the Lord thy God, that we die not: for we have added unto all our sins this evil, to ask us a king" (I Samuel 12:16-19).

Samuel's warning would have sounded something like this: *"If ye fear the Lord, and serve him, and obey his voice, and not rebel against the commandment of the Lord...and if your king will continue to follow the commandments of the Lord...but if ye obey not...if you do rebel...then the hand of the Lord will be strong against you...you have done this wickedness...but fear not...turn not aside...but from this point on serve the Lord with your whole heart and turn not aside from His precepts...for the Lord will not forsake His people for His great name's sake...remember it has pleased the Lord to make you His chosen and peculiar people..one more thing...God forbid if I should cease to pray for you day and night..for if you do any more wickedness you will be utterly consumed."*

Saul Rejected By God

According to the Word of the Lord, Saul led in seven military campaigns. (1) against the Ammonites at Jabesh-

Gilead; (2) against the Philistines; (3) several against Moab- Edom and Zobah; (4) against the Amalekites; (against the Philistines under Goliath ; (6) long and merciless pursuits against David; (7) against the Philistines at Mount Gilboa, which led to his death.

Despite an auspicious beginning, most of the remainder of Saul's reign was a tragic and disappointing affair fulfilling the prophecy of Samuel in Israel's demand for a king to rule in the place of God. By the time he had ruled for two years, he selected three thousand troops and took two thousand of them with him to Michmash and Munt Bethel while the other thousand stayed with his son, Jonathan, in Gibe-ah in the land of Benjamin. The rest of the men were sent home. At Geba Jonathan attacked and destroyed the garrison of the Philistines; Saul gathered his army again and met at Gilgal. But the Philistines gathered against Saul with a mighty army of horsemen, chariots and so many soldiers that they were as the sands of the sea. The men of Israel lost their courage and ran; they hid in caves, thickets, and coverts, or any other place where they could take cover from the invading Philistines. Some of them ran across the Jordan River and escaped into Gad and Gilead.

Samuel had told Saul to wait seven days for his arrival, but when he didn't come, and Saul saw his men disappearing in the night, he decided to sacrifice the burnt offering and the peace offerings himself. Saul intruded into the priest's office and lost the kingdom. When Samuel arrived, he questioned the actions of Saul for he knew by the Spirit of God what he had done.

"And Samuel said to Saul, Thou hast done foolishly: for thou hast not kept the commandment of the

Lord thy God which he commanded thee: for now would the Lord have established thy kingdom upon Israel for ever. But now thy kingdodm shall not continue: the Lord hath sought him a man after his own heart, and the Lord hath commanded him to be captain over his people, because thou hast not kept that which the Lord commanded thee" (I Samuel:13:13-14).

Saul had failed to wait for the prophet Samuel, and that was his first mistake. Next, he had pridefully intruded into the office of the priest which was punishable by death. At that point Samuel prophesied Saul's demise, and announced the reign of David when he said, *"a man after the heart of God."*

Next, Samuel told Saul to lead the soldiers in battle against the Amalekites, their cruel enemy in the south. He was to kill everything in sight, and God would be with Israel. Saul was obedient to all Samuel said except he spared the life of Agag, the king, and kept the best of the cattle. When he came back from this victorious battle, he met Samuel at Gilgal and lied to him. Then the Word of the Lord came to Samuel regarding the reign of Saul: *"It repenteth me that I have set up Saul to be king: for he is turned back from following me, and hath not performed my commandments. And it grieved Samuel; and he cried unto the Lord all night. And when Samuel rose early to meet Saul in the morning, it was told Samuel, saying Saul came to Carmel, and, behold, he set him up a place, and is gone about, and passed on, and gone down to Gilgal. And Samuel came to Saul: and Saul said unto him, Blessed be thou of the Lord: I have performed the commandment of the Lord. And Samuel said, What meaneth then this bleating of the sheep in mine ears, and the lowing of the oxen which I hear" (I Samuel 15:11-14).*

At that point Samuel told him what the Lord had told him to say. He reminded Saul that God had chosen him when he was as nothing in the land; not highly esteemed in the eyes of the people; and He had caused him to rise to fame to lead His people. Now, he had failed because he would not obey the voice of the Lord, nor his prophet. This rejection was, of course, a disastrous blow to King Saul who was enjoying his exploits of war by this time.

He became depressed and the spirit of madness fell upon him. To restore him to his sanity, a young man named David was called in to play the harp. David's music would sooth the king's troubled soul for a while; then he would again slip into a state of frenzied madness and lash out at the young musician.

Rebellion in the heart of Israel's king caused him to seek after the witch of Endor. He was by now a very desperate man. No amount of anointed music could salvage this broken ruler.

"And Samuel said, Hath the Lord as great delight in burnt offerings and sacrifices, as in obeying the voice of the Lord? Behold, to obey is better than sacrifice, and to hearken than the fat of rams. For rebellion is as the sin of witchcraft, and stubbornness is as iniquity and idolatry. Because thou hast rejected the word of the Lord, he hath also rejected thee from being king" (I Samuel 15:22-23).

Samuel spoke an object lesson that to obey God's commandments took precedent over any kind of sacrifice. In other words, sacrifices without submission are the same as witchcraft for both issue out of a heart full of pride and arragoncy. Rebellion against God is the root of the occult. Saul sought a place to repent. He begged Samuel to entreat the Lord in his behalf, but it was too late.

"And as Samuel turned about to go away, he laid hold upon the skirt of his mantle, and it rent. And Samuel said unto him, The Lord hath rent the kingdom of Israel from thee this day, and hath given it to a neighbour of thine, that is better than thou. And also the Strength of Israel will not lie nor repent: for he is not a man, that he should repent...And Samuel came no more to see Saul until the day of his death: nevertheless Samuel mourned for Saul: and the Lord repented that he had made Saul king over Israel" (I Samuel 15:27-35).

Chapter 8

DAVID AND GOLIATH

"And the Lord said unto Samuel, How long wilt thou mourn for Saul, seeing I have rejected him from reigning over Israel? Fill thine horn with oil, and go, I will send thee to Jesse the Bethlehemite: for I have provided me a king among his sons. And Samuel said, How can I go? if Saul hear it, he will kill me. And the Lord said, Take an heifer with thee, and say, I am come to sacrifice to the Lord. And call Jesse to the sacrifice, and I will show thee what thou shalt do: and thou shalt anoint unto me him whom I name unto thee" (I Samuel 16:1-3).

God chose Him a king among the sons of Jesse, the Bethlehemite, and as we read in Micah 5:2, "But thou, Bethlehem Ephrathah, though thou be little among the thousands of Judah, yet out of thee shall he come forth *unto me that is to be ruler in Israel, whose goings forth have been from of old, from everlasting.''* It is so true that God has chosen the foolish things of this world to confound the wise; He has chosen the weak things of this world to show forth His mighty power and glory. God goes to great lengths to see that no flesh shall glory in His Presence. It is apparent from the Bible record of the call of David that among the sons of Jesse, he was the least likely one to be anointed king of Israel. Samuel obeyed the Lord and traveled to Bethlehem to see the sons of Jesse; God had not told him the name of the next king; only the family from which he would be selected.

In this text we cannot cover all the beautiful types and shadows between David and our Blessed Lord Jesus; David was not only the ancestor of Christ, but in many respects, he was the most eminent personal type of Him in the Old Testament. In Isaiah 11:1-2, we read, *"And there shall come forth a rod out of the stem of Jesse, and a Branch shall grow out of his roots: And the spirit of the Lord shall rest upon him, the spirit of wisdom and understanding, the spirit of counsel and might, the spirit of knowledge and of the fear of the Lord;"*

In Jerimiah 23:5, we have the promise of the coming Messiah through the line of David, *"Behold, the days come, saith the Lord, that I will raise unto David a righteous Branch, and a King shall reign and prosper, and shall execute judgment and justice in the earth."* Christ in the New Testament is referred to as the *"Root and Offspring of David."*

True, Saul continued to occupy the throne for a time; but the Spirit of the Lord had departed. The important principle taught here is that many times a person, institution, or church is rejected by God secretly before the fact is made known to His people. A good example of this lies in the fact that at Calvary our Lord abandoned Judaism - yet the temple remained until it was destroyed by Titus in 70 A.D.

David Anointed by Samuel

"But the Lord said unto Samuel, Look not on his countenance, or on the height of his stature; becauses I have refused him: for the Lord seeth not as man seeth; for man looketh on the outward appearance, but the Lord looketh on the heart" (I Samuel 16:7).

Jesse passed seven of his sons before Samuel, and Samuel said to him, *"The Lord hath not chosen these"* (verse 10). Samuel asked Jesse if he had any more sons. There was yet one who was keeping the sheep at that moment. Samuel said, *"...fetch him."*

David was brought before the prophet Samuel as the last of Jesse's sons to stand before the Lord. In verse 5, we noted that Jesse and his seven sons had been sanctified, but David was not considered, so he stayed with the sheep. So insignificant was young David that he wasn't counted worthy to come to the ceremonies. But the Word of the Lord tells us that the *"counsel of the Lord ...shall stand" (Proverbs 19:21).*

Young David was ruddy, and of a beautiful countenance; he was handsome and vibrant - and the Lord said, *"...Arise, anoint him: for this is he" (verse 12).* Samuel took the horn of oil, and anointed David in the presence of his family, and the Spirit of the Lord came upon young

David from that day forward. May we take note that David was the eighth son, and eight means *"new beginnings."*

Samuel went back to his home in Ramah; then we are told that an evil spirit vexed Saul, because the Spirit of the Lord had departed from him. In the Old Testament the Hebrews believed that God sent *"evil spirits"* as a type of their judgment for sins, when in truth, any time God withdraws His presence, all sorts of evil can invade the lives of people who are arrogant and self-willed. *"But the spirit of the Lord departed from Saul, and an evil spirit from the Lord troubled him. And Saul's servants said unto him, Behold now, an evil spirit from God troubleth thee. Let our lord now command thy servants, which are before thee, to seek out a man, who is a cunning player on an harp: and it shall come to pass, when the evil spirit from God is upon thee, that he shall play with his hand, and thou shalt be well" (I Samuel 16:14-16).*

One of Saul's servants had heard of David's skill with the harp. David was sought out and brought to play before the king. David stood before Saul, his king, and he loved him greatly. He became his bodyguard. Whenever the evil spirit attacked Saul, David took his harp, and he played until the evil spirit departed. The powerful influence exerted by music upon the mind was well known even in those times.

We must not pass over lightly the fact that David was anointed then he entered into a position of service to his king. After his *"anointing"* came a season of testings. We must also mention that David was anointed three times, and so was our Blessed Lord. After the baptism and anointing of our Lord in the Jordan River, He immediately went into the wilderness to be *"tested"* for the devil had to be brought out into the open.

David And Goliath

Any child who has ever once attended a Sunday School class has heard the dramatic story of young David who slew the giant, and took off his head, (possible date was 1029 B.C.).

The Philistines apparently had decided that since Israel's God was no longer with them, it was time to make another all out attack. They camped between Socoh in Judah and Asekah in Ephes-dammim. Saul had a backup force at Elah Valley. There the Philistines and Israelis faced each other on opposite hills, with the valley below. Suddenly, a Philistine champion named Goliath from Gath appeared on the scene and faced Israel. He was over nine feet tall - a giant of a man - and he was wearing a bronze helmet, a two-hundred pound coat of mail,[1] bronze leggings, and he carried a bronze javelin several inches thick, tipped with a twenty-five pound iron spearhead; also, his armor bearer walked ahead of him carrying a gigantic shield. He shouted across to Israel, *"You do not need an entire army! Send me one man from among you, and if he is able to kill me, then we will be your servants. But if I kill him, then you will be our slaves. I challenge and defy the armies of Israel!"*

---

[1] "mail" flexible armor of interlinked metal rings.

Saul and all his men were dismayed and frightened. It must be noted that for forty days, twice a day, this giant paraded before the children of God and mocked them. Goliath speaks to us of the devil seeking to terrify the children of the Lord, and bring them into subjection to him by using scare tactics. He seeks whom he may devour.

Man's extremity is God's opportunity. But he does not always rush to deliver; *"He waits to be gracious" (Isaiah 30:18),* that His delivering hand may be more fully realized. Meanwhile, Jesse told David to take corn and bread to his brothers, and cheese was to be given to the captain. He told David to bring word back to him of their welfare. It would seem that each time the Israeli soldiers decided to advance upon the Philistines, Goliath stood up and growled, and they fled.

"And David spake to the men that stood by him, saying, What shall be done to the man that killeth this Philistine, and taketh away the reproach from Israel? for who is this uncircumcised Philistine, that he should defy the armies of the living God" (I Samuel 17:26)?

His brothers were furious with him, and accused him of being prideful and curious about what was going on with them. David told them they had no right to be angry with him. Others mocked and told Saul what the lad had said. Saul called for David, *"And David said to Saul, Let no man's heart fail because of him; thy servant will go and fight with this Philistine. And Saul said to David, Thou art not able to go against this Philistine to fight with him: for thou art but a youth, and he a man of war from his youth. And David said unto Saul, Thy servant kept his father's sheep, and there came a lion, and a bear, and took a lamb out of the flock: And I went out after him, and smote him, and delivered it out of his mouth: and when he arose against me, I caught him by his beard, and smote him, and slew him. Thy servant slew both the lion and the bear: and this uncircumcised Philistine shall be as one of them, seeing he hath defied the armies of the living God. And David said moreover, The Lord that delivered me out of the paw of the lion, and out of the paw of the bear, he will deliver me out of the hand of this Philistine. And Saul said unto David, Go, and the Lord be with thee" (I Samuel 17:32-37).*

Then Saul took his own armor and gave it to David; he had a bronze helmet and a coat of mail. David strapped on the sword, and took a step forward to check it out since he had never worn such a thing. He cried, *"I can't wear this heavy thing!"* And he took them off and chose five smooth stones out of the brook, and put them into his shepherd's bag and headed for the Philistine camp. When Goliath saw David, he roared, *"I am not a dog for you to come at me with a stick!"* And he cursed David by the name of his gods, and said he would feed David to the beasts of the field.

"And the Philistine said to David, Come to me, and I will give thy flesh unto the fowls of the air, and to the beasts of the field. Then said David to the Philistine, Thou comest to me with a sword, and with a spear, and with a shield: but I come to thee in the name of the Lord of hosts, the God of the armies of Israel, whom thou hast defied. This day will the Lord deliver thee into mine hand; and I will smite thee, and take thine head from thee; and I will give the carcases of the host of the Philistines this day unto the fowls of the air, and to the wild

beasts of the earth; that all the earth may know that the Lord saveth not with sword and spear: for the battle is the Lord's, and he will give you into our hands" (I Samuel 17:44- 47).

The Philistine rose to meet David, and David ran to meet him; he drew out a stone from his bag, and slung it and hit the Philistine giant in his forehead, and the giant fell to the ground. *"So David prevailed over the Philistine with a sling and with a stone..."* David ran to the Philistine, and since he had no sword, he pulled Goliath's from its sheath and killed him with it, and then cut off his head. When the Philistines saw their champion was dead they ran in fear.[2]

"I will praise thee, O Lord, with my whole heart; I will show forth all thy marvellous works. I will be glad and rejoice in thee: I will sing praise to thy name, O thou most High. When mine enemies are turned back, they shall fall and perish at thy presence. For thou hast maintained my right and my cause; thou satest in the throne judging right. Thou has rebuked the heathen, thou hast destroyed the wicked, thou hast put out their name for ever and ever" (Psalm 9:1-5).

We make note of the fact that after this battle, Saul made inquiries about young David; David appeared before the king with the head of Goliath in his hand. It was on that day that the soul of Jonathan, Saul's son, was bound to the soul of David; From that day on David did not go back to his home to live. Jonathan stripped himself of his robe, his garments, his sword and bow, and gave

---

[2]Possible location of Psalm 9.

them to David for he loved him with his whole heart. It was on that day that Jonathan and David made a covenant knitting their souls together. Each found in the other that flow of love they possibly failed to find in their own families. The word "knit" is the same Hebrew word used in Genesis 44:30, to express Jacob's love for Benjamin, his own son. Jonathan and David were "knit" together as family. The son of a king gave earthly possessions to a "shepherd" boy as proof of his love and admiration of him. Jonathan was "knit" together with the very one who would take the throne from him. David had already been anointed for it by Samuel under the Divine directions of the Lord. For many people this would have been occasion for jealousy, and hatred, but Jonathan loved David with all his heart. This must not be attributed to anything special in Jonathan, but must be ascribed to Him who has the rule over all creation. We remember it was the Lord who gave Joseph favor in the courts of Pharaoh in Egypt; it was the Lord God who sent the ravins to feed His prophet Elijah during hard times; and the same God and ruler of all, has promised Christians that He will never leave them helpless or desert them. *"The Lord is my shepherd; I shall not want. He maketh me to lie down in green pastures: he leadeth me beside the still waters. He restoreth my soul: he leadeth me in the paths of righteousness for his name's sake..." (Psalm 23:1-3).*

A Javelin In Saul's Hand

By now David was King Saul's special "right-hand" man. He went where he sent him, and obeyed orders down to the smallest detail. We see the hand of God in

David's earlier years of training. David became very popular with the people in this position. He was handsome and kind and loyal. Those who hope to rule must first learn to be obedient in the smaller things. It is much easier to abound that it is to be abased. With great Wisdom the Holy Spirit recorded that David *"behaved himself wisely,"* in all the matters of Saul. The prayer that should be on the lips of every born-again saint is that we conduct ourselves wisely in the affairs of our King. In Matthew 10:16, we are told, *"Be ye wise as serpents, and harmless as doves."* We do not compromise or hide, but we trust the Lord to keep and deliver us. We now point to the fact that the people chose Saul as king, but God chose David to take his place. In this God is working out all things for our good and His Glory.

David was too much magnified in the eyes of the common people and his troubles were just beginning. Some time after they returned from their victory over the Philistine, Saul went on a triumphal march through the cities of Israel, and to his dismay the women met him singing the praises of David: *"Saul has slain his thousands, but David his ten thousands."* Saul was furious. *"They said I had slain thousands, but to David they sang the praises of ten thousand. What more could he want but my kingdom?"*

"And it came to pass on the morrow, that the evil spirit from God came upon Saul, and he prophesied in the midst of the house: and David played with his hand, as at other times: and there was a javelin in Saul's hand. And Saul cast the javelin; for he said, I will smite David even to the wall with it. And David avoided out of his presence twice" (I Samuel 18:10-11).

Saul knew that the Lord was with David, and that He had departed from him. Again we are told that David behaved himself wisely in all his ways, and the Lord was with him. Such a scene we have before us. Saul went into a mad rage the next day; young David was summoned, and he ran into the room with his harp to sooth the nerves of the king. Quickly, the lad began to play for Saul; perhaps at that point, David did not realize that he was the object of the king's hate and envy. Twice he avoided the king's javelin, (here and again in 19:10). Proud men cannot bear to hear others praised in their presence.

As we read the Psalms, we realize that David prayed instead of taking revenge. After Saul's attempt upon young David's life, it is believed that Psalm 5 was to be inserted. In Psalm 5:8, we read, *"Lead me, O Lord, in thy righteousness because of mine enemies; make thy way straight before my face."*

Saul was more than jealous. He set himself to thwart God's purpose for Israel. He supposed that if he could take David's life, God would again visit him. Saul tried to make things happen, instead of resting his case with the Lord. That is the sad plight of a man who forgets his power is of God. Saul sent David into battles that he thought would rid him of his rival. When David returned, he offered his eldest daught in marriage to the young soldier; but when the time arrived for the wedding, Saul gave her to another man. His plots all failed, and he became driven by his jealous fury.

David Married Michal

Michal was Saul's other daughter, and she loved David. After a very successful battle with the Philistines, Saul gave her in marriage to David:

"Wherefore David arose and went, he and his men, and slew of the Philistines two hundred men; and David brought their foreskins, and they gave them in full tale to the king, that he might be the king's son in law. And Saul gave him Michal his daughter to wife. And Saul saw and knew that the Lord was with David, and that Michal Saul's daughter loved him. And Saul was yet the more afraid of David; and Saul became David's enemy continually. Then the princes of the Philistines went forth: and it came to pass, after they went forth, that David behaved himself more wisely than all the servants of Saul; so that his name was much set by" (I Samuel 18:27-30).

In this particular place, we have Psalm 12, *"Help, Lord; for the godly man ceaseth; for the faithful fail from among the children of men. They speak vanity every one with his neighbor: with flattering lips and with a douuble heart do they speak..."* (verses 1-2).

Jonathan Warned David

Saul told Jonathan and his servants that he planned the death of David; but Jonathan loved David, and he warned him of the king's plot. Jonathan spoke well of David to his father reviewing all of his exploits in behalf of the king, and added to that the fact that David had never sinned against the king. In that moment Saul heard the words of his son, and he swore that David would not be slain. But all this was a short-lived treaty.

Again there was war with the Philistines, and David slaughtered them and sent them running from him. Saul's efforts to get young David killed on the field of battle ended in a glorious victory. The people continued to esteem him highly. Saul once again had the evil spirit upon him, and once again David played his harp.

"And Saul sought to smite David even to the wall with the javelin; but he slipped away out of Saul's presesnce, and he smote the javelin into the weall: and David fled, and escaped into the night" (I Samuel 19:10).

David Becomes A Fugitive

Michal let David down through a window, and he escaped from the murderous king. Pursued by the hatred of Saul, he was forced to live like an outlaw. Michal told him he would not live to see morning if he did not get away that same night. After she helped him get down through the window, she took an idol and put it in the bed and covered it with blankets. When Saul's guards came to take him to the king, Michal told them he was too sick to get out of the bed so Saul ordered the men to bring him in the bed so he could kill him. We are reminded of our Lord Jesus and how the more the Pharisees persecuted Him, the more the people loved and sought after Him. Later, the more His witnesses were persecuted, the more the Gospel grew and prospered. How wonderful is the care of the Father for His Own. (Here is the possible location for Psalm 59).

David At Ramah

David had no choice but to run to Samuel and report what Saul had been doing to him. Likely David was running short of faith at this point and needed to be encouraged by the old prophet. Regardless of the sacredness of the place in which David had taken refuge, Saul sent his men to arrest him. Samuel took David to Naioth to live with him. When the soldiers came for David and saw Samuel and the other prophets prophesying, the Spirit of God came upon them and they also began to prophesy. More soldiers were sent by Saul when he learned what had happened to his first group; they too prophesied. Then Saul went to Ramah and demanded the whereabouts of David. Someone informed him that Samuel had taken David to Naioth in Ramah, so Saul started out for Naioth. But on the way the Spirit of God came upon Saul and he began to prophesy. He tore off his clothes and lay naked all day and all night prophesying with Samuel's prophets. Saul's men were astonished and asked if he too were one of Samuel's prophets. (This gave David plenty of time to escape).

After David fled from Naioth in Ramah, he found Jonathan. He asked him just what was his great sin that Saul would seek his life so many times. Jonathan at first denied that his father was trying to kill David; he claimed that the king always confided in him what he was about to do. David told Jonathan, *"...There is but a step between me and death" (I Samuel 20:3)*.

Jonathan at that point agreed to do anything he could for David. David had always been with Saul at the celebration of the new moon; but this time he would not go for fear of his life. He told Jonathan to tell Saul he had gone to visit his family. He told Jonathan if Saul became angry, then they would know his life was still in danger.

David asked for the confidence of Jonathan in the matter. He reminded him of their covenant.

"And Jonathan said, Far be it from thee: for if I knew certainly that evil were determined by my father to come upon thee, then would not I tell it thee" (I Samuel 20:9).

Arrow Of Warning

Jonathan and David agreed upon a plan. David hid in the field for three days during the new moon feast, while Jonathan check out the attitude of the king. Jonathan promised that he would talk with his father about David. David asked how he would know whether or not Saul was still angry.

"And Jonathan said unto David, O Lord God of Israel, when I have sounded my father about to morrow any time, or the third day, and, behold, if there be good toward David, and I then send not unto thee, and shew it thee; then Lord do so and much more to Jonathan: but if it please my father to do thee evil, then I will shew it thee, and send thee away, that thou mayest go in peace: and the Lord, be with thee, as he hath been with my father. And thou shalt not only while yet I live shew me the kindness of the Lord, that I die not: But also thou shalt not cut off thy kindness from my house for ever: no, not when the Lord that cut off the enemies of David every one from the face of the earth. So Jonathan made a covenant with the house of David, saying, Let the Lord even require it at the hand of David's enemies. And Jonathan caused David to swear again, because he loved him: for he loved him as he loved his own soul (I Samuel 20:12-17).

Jonathan told David to remain by the stone Ezel, and he would shoot three arrows on the side of it, pretending to hit a mark. Jonathan would bring a lad with him, and if he said to the lad, *"The arrows are on this side...you will know there is peace in the house; but if I say for him to search farther for the arrows, you will know there is trouble and you must flee."*

During the first day of the feast, the king did not ask about David. But the next day when he saw the place was still empty, he became furious and yelled out at Jonathan. He cursed Jonathan when he defended David, and screamed that David was after the throne that belonged to his son. Then Saul hurled the javelin at his own son; Jonathan left the table in a fierce anger, and the next morning he set out to warn David as he had promised. He shot the arrow - the boy began to run - when he reached the spot where he thought they fell, Jonathan yelled, *"No! Go on! They are ahead of you!"* The boy did not understand what was going on between Jonathan and David. After weeping for a while David reminded Jonathan that they had both entrusted each other and their children into the care of the Lord. So they parted going their separate ways.

David then headed for the city of Nob to see Ahimelech, the priest. David sought refuge in the house of God. David lied to the priest as to his mission. He asked the priest for a weapon and was given the sword of Goliath. By now he created quite a storm where ever he went.

From Nob he fled in fear of Saul to Achish, the king of Gath.

It would seem that David hoped he would not be recognized; here we note the absolute folly of David as he traveled to Gath with the *"sword of Goliath"* in his hand. One writer put it this way, "Common prudence might have taught him that if he sought the friendship of the Philistines, the sword of Goliath was not the most likely instrument to conciliate their favour." Jealous servants recognized him and began asking questions, so David pretended to be a mad man: he scrabbled on the doors of the gate, let his spittle fall down upon his beard, and kicked until the king sent him out of the court.

At this time in David's life the thirty-fourth Psalm was written by him. David, "king elect," was indeed running for fear of his life. There are times we might doubt his faith, but his fear did not rule his emotions as strongly as his love for God, and his respect for Saul as his king. In this Psalm the Holy Spirit gives us insight into the heart of the "king fugitive." In this Psalm we read of him blessing the Lord at all times: *"I sought the Lord and He heard me - he delivered me - the angel of the Lord encampeth round about them that fear Him..."* David had by then learned many valuable lessons, and he says, *"Come, ye children, hear me, and I will teach you to fear the Lord."* (Psalm 56 also inserted at this point).

Cave Of Adullam

David left Achish and escaped to the cave Adullam where his family joined him. Here we note the particular type of people who sought out David. They were the distressed, the discouraged, the outcasts. Later David got permission for his parents to live at Mizpeh in Moab under the protection of the king while he lived in the cave. Under the directions of the prophet Gad, David returned to

Judah; Saul heard of his return while he was sitting under an oak tree in Gibe-ah, playing with his spear, surrounded by his officers. Here he accused his men of not telling him all they knew of David and Jonathan. In response to those bitter words, Doeg, the Edomite, told of David's secret e visit to Ahimelech, and how he obtained food and a sword from the priest. The terrible results we find recorded in I Samuel 22:17- 23. Saul demanded his men to kill the priest and all his family; when they refused it was Doeg, the Edomite, who carried out the heinous crime. Apparently, Saul had set aside all over duties and was devoting all his time to the death of David. That day Doeg, by the orders of the king, killed eighty-five priests wearing their robes. (Possible location of Psalm 52,142-143).

"And David abode in the wilderness in strong holds, and remained in a mountain in the wilderness of Ziph. And Saul sought him every day, but God delivered him not into his hand" (I Samuel 23:14).

Chapter 9

THE REIGN OF DAVID

Saul returned from his battle with the Philistines one day, and he was informed that David had gone into the wilderness of Engedi; with three thousand special troops, he searched for him among the rocks and wild goats of the desert. Saul went into a cave to use the restroom, and to his dismay, David and his men were hiding there. David's men were filled with excitement for this surely was David's hour of victory over wicked Saul. *"Take him, David! This is what you have been waiting for!"*

David moved in on Saul and cut off his skirt; but his heart convicted him over his sudden and rash deed to his king. He told his men, *"...The Lord forbid that I should do this thing unto my master, the Lord's anointed, to stretch forth mine hand against him, seeing he is the anointed of the Lord"* (I Samuel 24:6).

David would not allow his men to raise a hand against Saul. When Saul left the cave, David followed him and cried, *"My Lord the king."* Saul turned and David bowed with his face to the ground and asked, *"Why do you listen when people tell you I mean you great harm? I have proven to you today that their words are far from true. I spared you, O king, to prove to you I will not touch the anointed of God."* When David finished speaking, King Saul began to cry.

"And he said to David, Thou art more righteous than I: for thou hast rewarded me good, whereas I have rewarded thee evil. And thou hast shown this day how that thou hast dealt well with me: forasmuch as when the Lord had delivered me into thine hand, thou killedst me not. For if a man find his enemy, will he let him go well away? wherefore the Lord reward thee good for that thou hast done unto me this day. And now, behold, I know well that thou shalt surely be king, and that the kingdom of Israel shall be established in thine hand. Swear now therefore unto me by the Lord, that thou wilt not cut off my seed after me, and that thou wilt not destroy my name out of my father's house. And David sware unto Saul. And Saul went home; but David and his men gat them up unto the hold" (I Samuel 24:17-22).

David and Abigail

Samuel died and while all Israel gathered to mourn and lament over him, David went into the wilderness of Paran. He had just confronted Saul and met the trial head on with mercy and meekness towards the greatest of his

The Reign Of David

enemies; in this part of our narrative, David once again faced a trial, one of a much milder nature, yet he acted in such a way as to reveal to each of us our own heart, proving, as another has said, no man stands a moment longer than Divine Grace upholds him.

David became furious with a farmer named Nabal who refused food to him and his men. By the same token, Nabal missed a golden opportunity to help "the anointed" of God. His answer to David was in the form of an insult and a flat out "no." David girded up his sword and made ready for all out war; but Nabal's wife, Abigail, got word of the incident and she did some fast thinking and moving.

"But one of the young men told Abigail, Nabal's wife, saying, Behold, David sent messengers out of the wilderness to salute our master, and he railed on them. But the men were very good unto us, and we were not hurt, neither missed we any thing, as long as we were conversant with them, when we were in the fields. They were a wall unto us both by night and day, all the while we were with them keeping the sheep. Now therefore know and consider what thou wilt do; for evil is determined against our master, and against all his household: for he is such a son of Belial, that a man cannot speak to him. Then Abigail made haste, and took two hundred loaves, and two bottles of wine, and five sheep ready dressed, and five measures of parched corn, and an hundred clusters of raisins, and two hundred cakes of figs, and laid them on asses" (Samuel 25:14-18).

David had vowed to slay every male child in the household; apparently, Abigail met him as he was on his way to carry out his threat. She jumped off her donkey, bowed herself to the ground, and fell at his feet. Nabal had insulted David as being a run-away slave, but his wife recognized him as her superior, her king, and she pleaded for the blame to be placed upon her. She accepted the blame for her husband's bad temper, and asked for forgiveness for her boldness in coming to him. She gave God the credit for having stayed the hand of David until she could reach him with her gifts.

"And David said to Abigail, Blessed be the Lord God of Israel, which sent thee this day to meet me: And blessed be thy advice, and blessed be thou, which hast kept me this day from coming to shed blood, and from avenging myself with mine own hand" (I Samuel 25:32-33).

God used Abigail to keep David from rewarding or answering the fool (Nabal) according to his folly (Proverbs 26:4). When she returned home she found Nabal was in the midst of a drunken party so she made no report to him. Several days later, when he had sobered, his wife told him what happened; he had a stroke and lay helpless then died at the hand of the Lord about ten days later.

When David heard the news of the death of Nabal, he sent his servants to get Abigail to be his wife. From the dust of the earth in humble submission before her king, to the throne of a queen, rose Abigail, to walk with him as his wife. David also married Ahino-am from Jezreel. In the meantime King Saul had forced Michal, David's wife, to marry a man from Gallim.

Touch Not The Anointed

Once again Saul set out in hot pursuit of David. There is a truth involved in this that must seek deep into our hearts. The way of the transgressor is hard says Proverbs 13:15; we know that the primary reference here is to the wicked, but the principle involved includes the redeemed. Another has said: God is exercising a moral government over the believer as well as the unbeliever, and He will no more wink at the sins of the one than He will of the other. David was saved by grace through faith apart from any good works-- and grace does not set aside the requirements of Divine Holiness, but it reigns through righteousness. Trials do not come upon us haphazardly. David was *"a man after the heart of God,"* because when he sinned, he was quick to repent. David realized he had acted rashly with Nabal.

David got word of the whereabouts of Saul, and slipped into his camp at night. Abishai wanted to kill Saul where he lay, but David refused to hear of it.

And David said to Abishai, Destroy him not: for who can stretch forth his hand against the Lord's anointed, and be guiltless? David said furthermore, As the Lord liveth, the Lord shall smite him; or his day shall come to die; or he shall descend into battle, and perish. The Lord forbid that I should stretch for mine hand against the Lord's anointed: but, I pray thee, take thou now the spear that is in his bolster, and the cruse of water, and let us go" (I Samuel 26:9-11).

David kept saying in his heart that someday he would surely perish at the hand of Saul. He fled to live among the Philistines. He was not welcome in his own land, and the Philistines hardly knew what to do with him.

The Witch Of Endor

"And it came to pass in those days, that the Philistines gathered their armies together for warfare, to

fight with Israel. And Achish said unto David, Know thou assuredly, that thou shalt go out with me to battle, thou and thy men. And David said to Achish, Surely thou shalt know what thy servant can do. and Achish said to David, therefore will I make thee keeper of mine head for ever" (I Samuel 28:1-2).

When Saul saw the troops of the Philistines, he was so scared that his heart almost stopped. He inquired of the Lord, but the Lord would not answer, so he disguised himself and sought the help of a woman who had a familiar spirit, (though he had banned all forms of witchcraft). We cannot enlarge on this particular point; but Saul deliberately sought the help of a "medium" which illustrates the fact that the apostates frequently commited the very sins they once denounced.

Death Of Saul

"Now the Philistines fought against Israel: and the men of Israel fled from before the Philistines, and fell down slain in mount Gilboa. And Philistines followed hard upon Saul and upon his sons; and the Philistines slew Jonathan, and Abinadab, and Melchi-shua, Saul's sons. And the battle was sore against Saul, and the archers hit him; and he was sore wounded of the archers. Then said Saul unto his armourbearer, Draw thy sword, and thrust me through therewith; lest these uncircumcised come and thrust me through, and abuse me. But his armourbearer would not; for he was sore afraid. Therefore Saul took a sword, and fell upon it. And when his armourberer saw that Saul was dead, he fell likewise upon his sword, and died with him. So Saul

died, and his three sons, and his armourbearer, and all his men, that same day together" (I Samuel 31:1-6).

Thus ended the career of the first king of Israel. We must take note that his great weakness was a spirit of rebellion and self-will. Saul killed himself in the presence of his enemies; When the Philistines foun the bodies of Saul and his sons, they cut off the head of the king, stripped off his armor and sent it back as a trophy to Philistia.

David lamented the death of Saul and Jonathan. He said, *"Saul and Jonathan were lovely and pleasant in their lives, and in their death they were not divided: they were swifter than eagles, they were stronger than lions"* (II Samuel 1:23).

Crowned At Judah

(1025-985 B.C. Chronology Bible)

The death of Saul left Israel without a king. David prayed to the Lord and was told to go to Hebron where the leaders of Judah would make him their king. David set up his kingdom in that ancient city, and for seven and one half years he ruled there while Ishbosheth, son of Saul, reigned over Israel. Pressed in between two references to the long war between his house and that of Saul is the record of his wives and his children. The puppet king, Ishbosheth, was assassinated, and David was offered the crown of the entire kingdom.

Jerusalem, The New Capital

One of David's first acts as king was to secure a suitable capital for his kingdom. Hebron was too far south and too closely associated with the tribes of Judah to be fully acceptable to the northern tribes. By the same token, a capital in the north would be offensive to Judah. He decided to set up 6. his kingdom headquarters in Jerusalem. The Israelites had never been able to conquer Jerusalem. The mountainous terrain on which it sat and its almost impregnable defenses had enabled it to withstand whatever attacks might have been made on it. By gaining control of this strategic city, David united Israel. The Canaanites had remained a "thorn" in Israel's side since the day of the conquest led by Joshua. The taking of Jerusalem and the final defeat of the Philistines were no small feats.

Jerusalem was situated in the center of western Palestine; it stood twenty-seven hundred feet above sea level and 4000 feet above the Dead Sea. *"Beautiful in elevation, the joy of the whole earth..." (Psalm 48:2).* For the first 2000 years of its existence this Canaanite town showed little development; then it became the capital of a succession of kings who ruled over the city itself and the small state around it. This conquest of Jebus by David set Jerusalem apart from all other cities. This new city was called "Zion" or The City of David."

The Ark Moved To Jerusalem

"Again, David gathered together all the chosen men of Israel, thirty thousand. And David arose, and went with all the people that were with him from Baale of Judah to bring up from thence the ark of God, whose name is called by the name of the Lord of hosts that dwelleth between the cherubims. They set the ark of God

upon a new cart, and brought it out of the house of Abinadab that was in Gibeah: and Ussah and Ahio, the sons of Abinadab, drave the new cart" (II Samuel 6:1-3).

The Ark of God on a "new cart" was patterned after the invention of the heathen. The "priests" of the Philistines had sent back the ark on a "new cart" drawn by oxen (I Samuel 6). Now, history has repeated itself. At Nachon's threshingfloor, Ussah put out his hand to stead the Ark, and he was struck dead by the Lord. David was displeased, and said, *"...How shall the ark of the Lord come to me?"* So David left the Ark in the house of Obed-edom for dthree months. Because of the Ark, the house of Obed-edom was bless greatly. So David brought the Ark from the house of Obed-edom into Jerusalem;. every six paces, they stopped and sacrificed to the Lord. They shouted and they sang all over Israel as they brought the Ark of the Lord into the City of David.

The Davidic Covenant

God sent peace upon the land, and Israel was no longer at war with the neighboring nations. As David sat in his house he said to Nathan the prophet: *"...See now, I dwell in an house of cedar, but the ark of God dwelleth within curtains"* (II Samuel 7:2)

Nathan told him to go ahead with his plans to build a house for the Lord, that the Lord was with him. But that night the Lord spoke to the prophet:

"Go and tell my servant David, Thus saith the Lord, Shalt thou build me an house for me to dwell in? Whereas I have not dwelt in any house since the time that I brought up the children of Israel out of Egypt,

even to this day, but have walked in a tent and in a tabernacle. In all the places wherein I have walked with all the children of Israel spake I a word with any of the tribes of Israel, whom I commanded to feed my people Israel, saying, Why build ye not me an house of cedar? Now therefore so shalt thou say unto my servant David, Thus saith the Lord of hosts, I took thee from the sheepcote, from following the sheep, to be ruler over my people, over Israel: And I was with thee whithersoever thou wentest, and have cut off all thine enemies out of thy sight, and have made thee a great name, like unto the name of the great men that are in the earth. Moreover I will appoint a place for my people Israel, and will plant them, that they may dwell in a place of their own, and move no more; neither shall the children of wickedness afflict them any more, as beforetime, And as since the time that I commanded judges to be over my people Israel, and have caused thee to rest from all thine enemies. Also the Lord telleth thee that he will make thee an house. And when thy days be fulfilled, and thou shalt sleep with thy fathers, I will set up thy seed after thee, which shall proceed out of thy bowels, and I will establish his kingdom. He shall build an house for my name, and I will stablish the throne of his kingdom for ever. I will be his father, and he shall be my son. If he commit iniquity, I will chasten him with the rod of men, and with the stripes of the children of men. But my mercy shall not depart away from him, as I took it from Saul, whom I put away before thee. And this thine house and thy kingdom shall be established for ever before thee: thy throne shall be established for ever" (II Samuel 7:5-16)

One has said how it is indeed beautiful to see the recently crowned monarch solicitious, not for the honor of his own majesty, but, for the glory of Him whom he served. It is not often that those in high places manifest such interest in spiritual things. Many of the Lord's people who are entrusted with considerable amounts of this world's goods are careless over the prospering of His cause. Today self indulgence has been crowned, and she sits conspiciously upon a coveted throne; too often we find separation from the world is a thing of the past and gratification of the flesh is the order of the times.

David was not trying to pay God for His mercy and goodness to him; he was concerned about a dwelling place for the Ark of God. In I Kings 8:18, we read, *"And the Lord said unto David my father, Whereas it was in thine heart to build an house unto My name, thou didst well that it was in thine heart."* God was pleased with the attitude of David's heart. Until God gives the instructions for His place of worship, a tent is better than a temple made from man's devising. Though God would not allow David to build a temple for Him, He let him know he was His beloved indeed. God announced rich blessings upon David and his family. From his seed should issue, according to the flesh, the promised Messiah and Mediator (verses 11-16). Thus, instead of David's building for the Lord a material and temporal house, the Lord would build for him a spiritual house which would abide forever. In this we see the "willing" mind is not only accepted, but is richly rewarded.

The Humility Of David

David sat before the Lord, and echoed the word of Moses of old when the Lord called him from the Midian desert and sent him to Egypt to deliver His people. Moses had been a sheepherder too long to feel adequate for the task. He said, *"Who am I that I should go to Pharaoh?"* In Psalm 131:1, we read, *"Lord, my heart is not haughty, nor mine eyes lofty: neither do I exercise myself in great matters, or in things too high for me."*

As he sat before the Lord in the Tabernacle, he poured out his feelings of genuine humility and abasement. *"And what one nation in the earth is like thy people, even like Israel, whom God went to redeem for a people to himself, and to make him a name, and to do for you great things and terrible, for thy land, before thy people, why thou redeemedst to thee from Egypt, from the nations and their gods? For thou hast confirmed to thyself thy people Israel to be a people unto thee for ever: and thou, Lord, art become their God. And now, O Lord God, the word that thou hast spoken concerning thy servant, and concerning his house, establish it for ever, and do as thou has said. And let thy name be magnified for ever, saying, The Lord of hosts is the God over Israel: and let the house of thy servant David be established before thee"* (II Samuel 7:23-26).

Bathsheba

At the very height of his power and fame, King David fell victim to temptation and in a moment of weakness committed a sin which brought shame and fearful consequences to himself and his family. This happened during a time of idleness. He was resting in the palace while his men were out fighting the Ammonites. Bathsheba was the wife of Uriah, one of the men in David's command. As

The Reign Of David

David walked upon his roof, he saw the woman bathing herself and called for her. Not only did he commit adultery with Uriah's wife, but he tried to cover up his sin by sending the man into the front lines of battle to be killed. After Uriah was dead, David married Bathsheba and a child was soon born to the union. When David sought forgiveness and was restored with the Lord, he expressed his relief and gratitude in the familiar word of Psalm 32. This sin and its consequences was tragically reflected in the life of the members of David's family for years to come.

Later David and Bathsheba had a son named Solomon; domestic troubles began to mount fast and thick. His son, Amnon, tricked his half-sister, Tamar, into the sin of fornication (incest), and her brother, Absalom, set out to avenge her honor. He killed Amnon, but fearing the anger of David, his father, he fled to Syria and remained in exile for a number of years. He was a favorite of his father, and David longed for his return. Unscrupulous Absalom was permitted to come back to Jerusalem "on probation," and he set into motion a wicked plot to steal the kingdom from David. By flattery and deceitful promises, he won the hearts of many of the people. He carefully picked his leaders; in time, he asked David for permission to go to Hebron to worship - there his henchmen met him and declared him to be king. David had to flee for his life. Psalm 63 inserted here.

We cannot cover all this story, but how touching were the final words of David over the death of his son, *"And the king was much moved, and went up to the chamber over the gate, and wept: and as he went, thus he said, O my son Absalom, my son, my son Absalmom! would God I had died for thee, O Absalom, my son, my son!" (II Samuel 18:33).*

Chapter 10

THE REIGN OF SOLOMON

In II Samuel seven, we read David' prayer; in II Samuel 22, we have possibly the most beautiful praise and worship chapter in the Bible, spoken by David towards the end of his life and reign as king over Israel. In II Samuel seven, David cried out, *"Who am I?"* But in II Samuel 22, he proclaimed, *"Who is God?"* and answered, *"The Lord is my rock, and my fortress, and my deliverer; The God of my rock; in him will I trust: he is my shield, and the horn of my salvation, my high tower, and my refuge, my saviour; thou savest me from violence. I will call on the Lord, who is worthy to be praised: so shall I be saved from mine enemies...In my distress I called upon the Lord, and cried to my God: and he did hear my voice out of his temple, and my cry did enter into his ears...He brought me forth also into a large place:*

he delivered me, because he delighted in me...For thou art my lamp, O Lord: and the Lord will lighten my darkness. For by thee I have run through a troop: by my God have I leaped over a wall. As for God, his way is perfect; the word of the Lord is tried: he is a buckler to all them that trust in him. For who is God, save the Lord? and who is a rock, save our God? God is my strength and power: and he maketh my way perfect. He maketh my feet like hinds' feet: and setteth me upon my high places...The Lord liveth; and blessed be my rock; and exalted be the God of the rock of my salvation...Therefore I will give thanks unto thee, O Lord, among the heathen, and I will sing praises unto thy name. He is the tower of salvation for his king: and showeth mercy to his anointed, unto David, and to his seed for ever."

In II Samuel 23 and 24, we have the last words and deeds of King David. Our placement of the Psalms is by no means complete. In chapter 24, we learn that David numbered the people, and because this thing angered the Lord, he gave David a choice of his punishment. In I Chronicles 21, we learn, by cross reference, that it was Satan who stood up against Israel, and provoked David to number Israel. Joab tried to talk the king out of such a ridiculous idea. Nevertheless, David insisted that the people be numbered, and his subjects obeyed their king. This rebellious act of pride cost Israel 70,000 men; then David cried out to the Lord and repented, and the death angel stayed his hand.

Solomon Anointed
(About 971 B.C.)

David was old and unable to handle the affairs of state any longer. His natural heat was so wasted that no clothes could keep him warm. It would have been heartbreaking to see this once valiant and active man so wasted and confined to the bed. In the book of Haggai, we are warned to consider our ways at all times: *"Ye have sown much, and bring in little; ye eat, but ye have not enough; ye drink, but ye are not filled with drink; ye clothe you, but there is none warm; and he that earneth wages earneth wages to put it into a bag with holes"* (1:6).

The three oldest sons of David were dead; Adonijah, the fourth, declared himself the next king of Israel. He got a strong body-guard, and the support of the high priest, Abiathar and Joab, and launched an all out effort to take the throne. He almost succeeded, but Nathan, the prophet, consulted with Bathsheba, and informed her of the plot and suggested that she should approach David and let him know.

Adonijah went to En-rogel where he sacrificed sheep, oxen, and fat young goats at the *"serpent's stone."* He called the other sons of David, and all the royal officials of Judah to come to his coronation. He failed to invite Nathan, and his brother, Solomon.

Bathsheba appeared before the king and reminded him that he had vowed to her that Solomon would be their next king; then she told David about Adonijah. While she was yet talking, Nathan, the prophet, appeared. He informed David that it was no longer just a plot. Adonijah had crowned himself king.

David called again for Bathsheba to stand before him. He renewed his vow that Solomon was to be their next king. He called for Zadok the priest, Nathan the prophet, and Benaiah, to come for his orders.

(1) Call Solomon, Zadok the priest, Nathan the prophet, and Benaiah;

(2) Take them to Gihon;

(3) Put Solomon on my personal mule;

(4) There he is to be anointed King of Israel;

(5) Blow the trumpets

(6) Shout, "Long live King Solomon!"

(7) Bring him back and place him upon my throne.

When Adonijah, and his banqueting guest, heard the noise, and learned of the new king, they fled in panic. Adonijah rushed into the Tabernacle and grabbed the horns of the altar for safety. Solomon summoned him, and said, *"Go on home in peace."*

"Now the days of David drew nigh that he should die; and he charged Solomon his son, saying, I go the way of all earth: be thou strong therefore, and show thyself a man; And keep the charge of the Lord thy God, to walk in his ways, to keep his statutes, and his commandments, and his judgments, and his testimonies, as it is written in the law of Moses, that thou mayest prosper in all that thou doest, and whithersoever thou turnest thyself: That the Lord may continue his word which he spake concerning me, saying, If thy children take heed to their way, to walk before me in truth with all their heart and with all their soul, there shall not fail thee (said he) a man on the throne of Israel...So David slept with his fathers, and was buried in the city of David. and the days that David reigned over Israel were forty years: seven years reigned he in Hebron, and

thirty and three years reigned he in Jerusalem. Then sat Solomon upon the throne of David his father; and his kingdom was established greatly" (I Kings 2:1-4, 10-12).

Adonijah Put To Death

Adonijah had once been spared by King Solomon; but he became involved in another scheme to overthrow the king, and orders were sent out that he should be executed along with Joab who had been guilty of many murders during David's reign. We must keep in mind that Solomon was dealing with heartless and unscrupulous men who would plunder and kill to rise to power.

The Wisdom Of Solomon

While Solomon and his officials were at Gibeon, six miles north of Jerusalem, offering sacrifices, the Lord appeared to him in a dream and said, *"Ask what I shall give thee."*

"And Solomon said, Thou hast shown unto thy servant David my father great mercy, according as he walked before thee in truth, and in righteousness, and in uprightness of heart with thee; and thou hast kept for him this great kindness, that thou hast given him a son to sit on his throne, as it is this day. And now, O Lord my God, thou hast made thy servant king instead of David my father: and I am but a little child: I know not how to go out or come in. And thy servant is in the midst of thy people which thou hast chosen, a great people, that cannot be numbered nor counted for multitude.

Give therefore thy servant an understanding heart to judge thy people, that I may discern between good and bad: for who is able to judge this thy so great a people" (I Kings 3:6-9).

"And God said unto him, Because thou hast asked this thing, and hast not asked for thyself long life; neither hast asked riches for thyself, nor hast asked the life of thine enemies; but hast asked for thyself understanding to discern judgment; Behold, I have done according to thy words: lo, I have given thee a wise and an understanding heart; so that there was none like thee before thee, neither after thee shall any arise like unto thee. And I have also given thee that which thou hast not asked, both riches, and honour: so that there shall not be any among the kings like unto thee all thy days. And if thou wiult walk in my ways, to keep my statutes and my commandments, as thy father David did walk, then I will lengthen thy days" (I Kings 3:11-14).

"But seek ye first the kingdom of God and His righteousness and all these things shall be added unto you" (Matthew 6:33).

King Solomon had assumed his responsibilities at at time when the nation was at its greatest peak. He used about the same plan of organization for his government as that of his father, David; but the cabinet was enlarged and more departments added. He had made an alliance with Pharaoh, the king of Egypt, and married one of his daughters. He brought her to Jerusalem to live in the city of David until he could finish building his palace, the temple, and the wall around the city.

Solomon loved the Lord, but he continued to sacrifice in the hills and to offer incense there. But in the spring of the fourth year of his reign, he started the actual construction of the Temple. It is interesting to note that this was 480 years after the children of Israel were delivered from Egyptian bondage.

King Solomon ruled from the Euphrates River to the land of the Philistines, and down to the borders of Egypt, and these conquered people continued to pay taxes to him throughout his lifetime. However, Israel and Judah continued to live in peace and contentment all his days. Each family had a house and a garden.

The daily food requirements for King Solomon's palace were:

195 bushels of fine flour

390 bushels of meal

10 oxen from the fattening pens

20 pasture-fed cattle

100 sheep or deer, gazelles, roebucks, and plump fowl.

The Temple

"Ye are the temple of God, and the Spirit of God dwelleth in you" (I Corinthians 3:16).

"And, behold, I purpose to build an house unto the name of the Lord my God, as the Lord spake unto David my father, saying, Thy son, whom I will set upon thy throne in thy room, he shall build an house unto my name" (I Kings 5:5).

Probably the most successful of Solomon's political measures was his treaty with Hiram the king of Tyre.

Hiram had strong ties with King David, and he was very careful to maintain these desirable ties with King Solomon. He supplied Solomon with cedar and cypress for his building of the Temple. He personally supervised much of the work. The two kings also cooperated in a shipping venture which opened up extensive trade with the lands to the south. Also, Solomon controlled the major caravan routes of the northern Near East and was able not only to trade with these caravans, but to collect sizable taxes in return for the use of the routes. It is quite probable that the famous visit of the Queen of Sheba was to discuss agreement about trade routes in the south. The Kingdom of Sheba (Sabeans) was located in southern Arabia and had control of the valuable spice and incense (myrrh and frankincense) trade of the region.

The building of the Temple was the first great work of Solomon after the establishment of his throne; he entered upon this work in his third year of reign, and completed it in the eleventh year of his reign. It was a work of unequalled magnificence. (Completion date coincided with *"Feast of the Tabernacles"* celebration).

Temple Materials And Workmen

King Solomon drafted 30,000 laborers from all over Israel and sent them to Lebanon on a rotation basis. Each man was in Lebanon a month and at home two months. The Temple was ninety feet long, thirty feet wide, and forty-five feet high. All along the front of the Temple was a porch thirty feet long and fifteen feet deep. These trees were cut from the forests of Lebanon, then floated down the coast to Joppa; and from there it was taken overland up the mountains to Jerusalem. The stone was taken from quarries near Jerusalem, cut and fitted , and then moved to the building site. The materials for the Temple were carefully prepared beforehand so that when they were assembled the great building was put up "without the noise of hammer." All the metals were imported. The Temple itself consisted of three general sections: the porch, which was some fifteen feet deep, thirty feet wide, and forty-five feet high; the Holy Place, which was thirty feet wide, forty-five feet high and sixty feet long. It was made of hewn stone, with cedar wainscoting and overlaid with gold. In this room was placed the Golden Altar of Incense, the table of Shewbread, and the ten Golden Candlesticks. The Holy of Holies on the west end was a perfect cube, thirty feet in height, length and width. It was separated from the Holy Place by a beautiful veil. It contained the Ark and the huge Cherubim. The Temple without the Ark, thou magnificently built, would be like the body without the soul.

We should note that eighty thousand workmen were employed in the mountains as hewers of wood, seventy thousand more as carriers, while three thousand-three hundred more were overseers; plus the thirty-thousand already mentioned. These men worked for years on Solomon's stupendous undertakings.

The Site Of The Temple

Solomon's Temple was erected on Mount Moriah, the sacred spot where Abraham offered up Isaac, and where Araunah so generously offered his threshing floor, his oxen and his implements, to sacrifice to the Lord.

Temple Dedication

The work was done and the Temple was ready for its dedication to the Lord. There was no hurry so they calmly waited until the proper season, the feast of the Tabernacles. Then all Israel gathered from all over the vast empire to witness this magnificent event in their national history.

"And all the elders of Israel came, and the priests took up the ark. And they brought up the ark of the Lord, and the tabernacle of the congregation, and all the holy vessels that were in the tabernacle, even those did the priests and the Levites bring up. And King Solomon, and all the congregation of Israel, that were assembled unto him, were with him before the ark, sacrificing sheep and oxen, that could not be told nor numbered for multitude. And the priests brought in the ark of the covenant of the Lord unto his place, into the oracle of the house, to the most holy place, even under the wings of the cherubims. For the cherubims spread forth their two wings over the place of the ark, and the cherubims covered the ark and the staves thereof above. And they drew out the staves, that the ends of the staves were seen out in the holy place before the oracle, and they were not seen without: and there they are unto this day. There was nothing in the ark save the two tables of stone, which Moses put there at Horeb, when the Lord made a covenant with the children of Israel, when they came out of the land of Egypt. And it came to pass, when the priests were come out of the holy place, that the cloud filled the house of the Lord, so that the priests could not stand to minister because of the cloud: for the glory of the Lord had filled the house of the Lord" (I Kings 8:3-11).

King Solomon stepped forward arrayed in all the priestly splendor of his day. A most solemn hush fell over the crowd mingled with awe and unutterable joy, and Jehovah was in their midst to dedicate His Own Temple. Of Solomon, A. B. Simpson wrote, *"As soon as he recovered from the deep prostration of this glorious manifestation he proceeded to utter the wonderful prayer of dedication, which seemed inspired of the Holy Ghost and which covered all the future of the people. This was followed by the sacrifice on an enormous scale of no less than twenty-two thousand oxen and one hundred and twenty thousand sheep, until the altar became too small and the whole court was transformed into a place of sacrifice. Then the fire of God came down from heaven and consumed the sacrifices, and the glory of the Lord filled the house, and as the people witnessed the manifest presence and power of God they fell upon their faces and worshiped the Lord, saying, 'For He is good, His mercy endureth forever."*

Second Visit From God

After Solomon had finished with all his building projects, the Lord appeared to him the second time, and covered some very weighty matters with the king of Israel.

"...I have heard thy prayer and thy supplication, that thou hast made before me: I have hallowed this house, which thou hast built, to put my name there for ever; and mine eyes and mine heart shall be there perpetually. And if thou wilt walk before me, as David thy father walked, in integrity of heart, and in uprightness, to do according to all that I have commanded thee, and

will keep my statutes and my judgments: Then I will establish the throne of thy kingdom upon Israel for ever, as I promised to David thy father, saying, There shall not fail thee a man upon the throne of Israel. But if ye shall at all turn from following me, ye or your children, and will not keep my commandments and my statutes which I have set before you, but go and serve other gods, and worship them: Then will I cut off Israel out of the land which I have given them; and this house, which I have hallowed for my name, will I cast out of my sight; and Israel shall be a proverb and a byword among all people: And at this house, which is high, every one that passeth by it shall be atonished, and shall hiss; and they shall say, Why hath the Lord done thus unto this land, and to this house? And they shall answer, Because they forsook the Lord their God, who brought forth their fathers out of the land of Egypt, and have taken hold upon other gods, and have worshipped them, and served them: therefore hath the Lord brought upon them all this evil" (I Kings 9:3-9).

Solomon's Downfall

King Solomon gathered for himself seven hundred wives, and three hundred concubines besides the Egyptian princess. Most of them were from nations where idols were worshipped. God had warned him of the consequences, but he did it his way and refused to destroy their idols. He went so far as to build a temple on the Mount of Olives, across the valley from Jerusalem, for Chemosh, the depraved god of Moab, and another for Molech, the vile god of the Ammonites. He built several temples dedicated to the worship of foreign gods. This was the beginning of the end for Solomon. His own people were weary of the heavy burden of taxes so the king could support his wives and luxurious court, and they finally rebelled. The surrounding areas who had been under Solomon's oppressive rule, gathered together to rebel against him. God was angry with him for he had turned away from the God of Israel to serve strange gods. Then the Lord spoke the saddest words ever to be recorded in the history of his people: *"...Solomon, Forasmuch as this is done of thee, and thou hast not kept my covenant and my statutes, which I have commanded thee, I will surely rend the kingdom from thee, and will give it to thy servant. Notwithstanding in thy days I will not do it for David thy father's sake: but I will rend it out of the hand of thy son. Howbeit I will not rend away all the kingdom; but will give one tribe to thy son for David my servant's sake, and for Jerusalem's sake which I have chosen"* (I Kings 11:11-13).

Solomon in his old age became entangled with the spirit of pride and lust which teaches that we must not depend upon our own strength. This man whose own proverbs warned young men over and over not be become ensnared by foolish women and red wine, was himself wretchedly bewitched by heathen women. It is easier to see a mischief, and to show it to others, than to turn aside from it ourselves. The Lord stirred up adversaries against Solomon for the rest of his days. As long as he lived by the precepts of God, Solomon knew no danger; but he forgot the God of his father, David, and the price was his kingdom. He reigned over all Israel forty years; then he slept with his fathers, and was buried in the city of David; Rehoboam, his son took the throne.

Chapter 11

KINGDOM DIVIDED

In the year 922 B.C., the empire of David and Solomon divided into two kingdoms. The northern portion kept the name Israel, and the southern portion took the name of its largest tribe, Judah. After two hundred years of troubled existence, the ten northern tribes were carried into Assyrian captivity (722 B.C.), and "passed forever" from the pages of history. The southern kingdom lasted some one hundred and fifty years, then gave way to the mighty armies of Nebuchadnezzar and went into Babylonian captivity in 586 B.C. During all that time there were only brief periods of peace and prosperity; but the glory that had once belonged to Israel in the days of King Solomon was never again realized. Much of this history is skipped over by Bible students because one finds it difficult to follow the reign of one bad king after another.

The narrative skips back and forth from Judah to Israel, and again, is difficult to follow. It is easier to study this portion either by chart or by taking one kingdom at a time with the prophets connected with the king in whose reign they prophesied.

The split between the northern and the southern tribes marked the total fall of the Israelite empire. The main events of this important period of Hebrew history are recorded in the books of Kings and in the books of Chronicles. We will list the kings of Judah and the kings of Israel:

Kings Of Judah	Length of Reign	Prophets
Rehoboam (Solomon's son)	17	Iddo-Shemaiah
Abijah	3	
Asa	41	Hannai, Azariah
Jehoshaphat	25	Jehu, Eliezer, Jahaziel
Jehoram	8	Elisha
Ahaziah (slain)	1	
Athaliah (queen-slain)	6	
Joash (slain)	40	Elisha
Amaziah (slain)	29	
Ussiah	52	Zechariah Isaiah
Jotham	16	Isaiah, Micah
Ahaz	16	Isaiah, Micah
Hezekiah	29	Isaiah, Micah
Manasseh	55	
Amon (slain)	2	
Josiah (slain)	31	
Jehoahaz (Egypt)	3 months	
Jehoiakim	11	
Jehoiachin (Egypt)	3 months	

Zedekiah (Babylon)	11	
Jeroboam I	22	Iddo, Shemaiah
Nadab (slain)	2	
Baasha	24	Jehu
Elah (slain)	2	
Zimri (suicide)	7 days	
Omri	12	
Ahab (slain)	22	Elijah, Micaiah
Ahaziah (accident)	2	
Jehoram (slain)	12	Elisha
Jehu	28	Elisha
Jehoahaz	17	Elisha
Jehoash	16	
Jeroboam II	41	Jonah, Amos Hosea
Zachariah (slain)	6 months	Hosea
Shallum (slain)	1 month	Hosea
Menahem	10	Hosea
Pekahiah (slain)	2	Hosea
Pekah (slain)	20	Hosea, Micah
Hoshea (prison)	9	Hosea, Micah

We mention again at this point the downfall of Israel, the northern kingdom. The collapse came with the downfall of Samaria, besieged by the Assyrians from 725-722. The brief record in the Bible of this important event in the history of the Hebrew people is given in II Kings 17:5-6): *"Then the king of Assyria came up throughout all the land, and went up to Samaria, and besieged it three years. In the ninth year of Hoshea, the king of Assyria took Samaria and carried Israel away unto Assyria, and placed them in Halah, and on the Habor, the river of Gozan, and in the cities of the Medes."*

Nebuchadnezzar destroyed Jerusalem and the southern kingdom fell into his hands. This capativity lasted seventy years; but with the rise of King Cyrus to the throne, things begin to look better once again for God's people. *"Thus saith Cyrus king of Persia, All the kingdoms of the earth hath the Lord God of heaven given me; and he hath charged me to build him an house in Jerusalem, which is Judah. Who is there among you of all his people? the Lord his God be with him, and let him go up" (II Chronicles 36:23).*

CHAPTER 12

ELIJAH THE TISHBITE

At this point we go back into the history of Israel to view the lives of two of the most poignant yet colorful prophets of all times, Elijah and Elisha.

Elijah Before Ahab

"And Elijah the Tishbite, who was of the inhabitants of Gilead, said unto Ahab, As the Lord God of Israel liveth, before whom I stand, there shall not be dew nor rain these years, but according to my word. And the word of the Lord came unto him, saying, Get thee hence, and turn thee eastward, and hide thyself by the brook Cherith, that is before Jordan. And it shall be, that thou shalt drink of the brook; and I have commanded the ravens to feed thee there" (I Kings 17:1-4).

We do not know about the early years of King Ahab who was one of Israel's most famous (or infamous) kings. His history is not an easy one to follow; he was married to Jezebel who was a most ardent devotee of Baal worship, and she was bent on destroying the worship of Jehovah in Israel and replace it with her own gods. She used all kinds of unscrupulous means, which included persecutions and death. She destroyed many of the prophets of God, Just when the situation looked hopeless, God brought Elijah (My God Is Power) upon the scene. We need we realize the importance of the meaning of his name. God says that He is our power and our strength, which means we move and have our being in the strength of the Lord Who is our peace. As long as the kings moved and ruled in the power and wisdom of the Lord, their kingdom prevailed; but when they moved and ruled in the power of human strength, they failed utterly.

When Elijah arrived on the scene of Israel's history, the process of Divine Revelations commenced again, having been suspended since the time of Joshua. As a true prophet of God, Elijah knew that the heart of God was turned in behalf of His people. Though we know very little of his background, God called him to stand before kings as a prophet of judgment and warning. When he confronted Ahad, he condemned him for the altars that he had built for Jezebel's gods, and announced a famine all over the land.

Elijah At Cherith

In obedience to Divine instructions from the Lord, Elijah traveled east to Cherith Brook at the place where it enters the River Jordan. He hid *"under the shadow of the Almighty."* The ravens were commanded to feed him, and he drank his water from the brook. When the brook dried up, due to lack of rain, the Lord spoke to Elijah and told him to move on. *"Whatsoever the Lord pleased, that did he in heaven, and in earth, in the seas, and all deep places" (Psalms 135:6).*

Elijah At Zarephath

The Brook was dried up but God's tender care and love for those who serve Him will never fail or slacken. In the meantime, King Ahab had searched "high and low" for the prophet to demand that he bring rain upon the earth.

"And the word of the Lord came unto him saying, Arise,, get thee to Zarephath, which belongeth to Zidon, and dwell there: behold, I have commanded a widow woman there to sustain thee" (I Kings 17:8-9). Much has been written about the miracles of Elijah in Zarephath. The word Zarephath means *"refining"* or *"smelting furnace."* Jezebel was from this country which meant that Elijah had to travel through country ruled by Ahab. In Zarephath two most important miracles took place. As Elijah came to the gate of the city, he met a widow who was gathering sticks. He asked her for water and food. He had traveled some one hundred miles from Cherith to Zarephath through barren and dry land. God always works on both ends of the line to achieve His purpose. The Bible did not give her a name, but the Holy Spirit makes it clear to us that this was the woman God had in mind to receive His blessings. *"...I have not a cake, but an handful of*

meal in a barrel, and a little oil in a cruse: and, behold, I am gathering two sticks, that I may eat it, and die. And Elijah said unto her, Fear not; go and do as thou hast said: but make me thereof a little cake first, and bring it unto me, and after make for thee and for thy son. For thus saith the Lord God of Israel, The barrel of meal shall not waste, neither shall the cruse of oil fail, until, the day that the Lord sendeth rain upon the earth" (I Kings 17:12-14).*

Elijah spoke the Word of the Lord in faith to the woman; but in order for her to receive the blessings, she had to respond to his words. In the natural things looked next to impossible for both Elijah and the widow. Gove God something to work with, and He is responsible for the miracles. He will provide for the hundred fold return on what we give to Him. With God all things are possible. It only takes a little oil, a little water, and the God kind of faith to receive from the Lord.

"O fear the Lord, ye his saints: for there is no want to them that fear him" (Psalms 34:9).

"He that hath pity upon the poor lendeth unto the Lord; and that which he hath given will he pay him again" (Proverbs 19:17).

Jesus made reference to this particular story when he said, *"...Verily I say unto you, No prophet is accepted in his own country. But I tell you of a truth, many widows were in Israel in the days of Elias, when the heaven was shut up three years and six months, when great famine was throughout all the land; but unto none of them was Elias sent, save unto Sarepta, a city of Sidon, unto a woman that was a widow" (Luke 4:24-26).*

Many widows were in Israel in those days - yet Elijah was sent to a gentile city - so he became (says Dr. Lightfoot) the first prophet of the Gentiles. Israel had corrupted themselves with the idolatries of other nations and become worse than they.

Later, Elijah was empowered by the Spirit of God to raise the widow's son from death. We note three very distinct characteristics in Elijah. He was totally empied of self, and obedient to the will of God; he lived in total obedience to the Father's will; and he lived by the Word of the Lord, and not by his own word or thoughts.

After three years of famine, the Word of the Lord came to Elijah telling him it was time for him to face Ahab again for rain was coming upon the earth. He set out for Samaria to find Ahab and met Obadiah, Ahab's servant, on the way. Obadiah's reaction to Elijah is somewhat amusing. He fell on his face before Elijah in an attitude of worship; Elijah told him to go tell the king, *"...Behold, Elijah is here."* The servant exclaimed, *"What is my sin that I should have to do such a thing? Ahab will kill me! He has sent messages to every king asking if they are hiding you! And you order me to go tell him you are here? Just as soon as I deliver the message, the Spirit of the Lord will lift you up and take you away, and when Ahab cannot find you, he will slay me. Have mercy, for I myself have feared the Lord from my youth. I know someone must have told you how I hid the prophets of the Lord from Jezebel in a cave and feed them with bread and water. And now you tell me to go tell Ahab you are here! he will kill me!"*

Elijah gave the servant his word that he would not disappear; so Obadiah delivered the message and Ahab met with Elijah, and said, *"Aren't you the prophet that has troubled Israel for so long?" "...I have not troubled Israel; but thou, and thy father's house, in that ye have forsaken the commandments of the Lord, and thou hast followed Baalim. Now therefore send, and gather to me all Israel unto mount Carmel, and the prophets of Baal four hundred and fifty, and the prophets of the groves four hundred, which eat at Jezebel's table" (I Kings 18:18-19).*

Let God Arise

It was time for a showdown between the gods of Baalim and the God of Israel. Ahab had no choice but to call for a meeting of his false prophets for he needed rain, and he knew that Elijah had the mind of God. This was a demonstration of the power of God over the hearts of men. In Proverbs 21:1, we read, *"The king's heart is in the hand of the Lord, as the rivers of water: he turneth it whithersoever he will."*

The meeting place was Mount Carmel, located on the northwest corner of Palestine; it rises out of the Mediterranean Sea - the peak being about 1740 feet above sea level; a little southeast of it is a great plateau about 1680 feet in altitude. Mount Carmel (the Mount of God) has been famous since antiquity for its luxuriant growth. Its garden-like lovliness was sacred to the Canaanites as the sanctuary of the *"Baal of Heaven,"* a name applied to Hadad, the life-giving god of the mountains, the lord of the rain, and of the lightning. From his sacred abode at Carmel, Hadad commanded the distant horizon and protected seafares. (The tribe of Asher inherited Mount Carmel). *"And Elijah came unto all the people, and said,*

How long halt ye between two opinions? if the Lord be God, follow him: if Baal, then follow him. And the people answered him not a word. then said Elijah unto the people, I, even I only, remain a prophet of the Lord; but Baal's prophets are four hundred and fifty men" (I Kings 18:21-22).

Israel had reached a sad state of affairs when one prophet of God stood alone challenging hundreds of the gods of Baal. Elijah called for two young bulls; one for each side; it was to be cut into pieces and placed on the wood of the altar without fire. He told the prophets of Baal to pray to their god and he would pray to the God of Israel. The false prophets prepared the sacrifice, and prayed all morning, shouting to their gods. No answer came; they began to dance around the altar, but nothing happened.

Elijah began to mock them. They shouted even louder, and cut themself until the blood ran which was their custom, but nothing happened. Then Elijah called to the people: *"...Come near unto me. And all the people came near unto him. And he repaired the altar of the Lord that was broken down. And Elijah took twelve stones, according to the number of the tribes of the sons of Jacob, unto whom the word of the Lord came, saying, Israel shall be thy name: And with the stones he built an altar in the name of the Lord: and he made a trench about the altar, as great as would contain two measures of seed. And he put the wood in order, and cut the bullock in pieces, and laid him on the wood, and said, Fill four barrels with water, and pour it on the burnt sacrifice, and on the wood. And he said, Do it the second time. and they did it the second time. And he said, Do* it the third time. and they did it the third time. And the water ran round about the altar; and he filled the trench also with water. And it came to pass at the time of the offering of the evening sacrifice, that Elijah the prophet came near, and said, Lord God of Abraham, Isaac, and of Israel, let it be known this day that thaou art God in Israel, and that I am thy servant, and that I have done all these things at thy word. Hear me, O Lord, hear me, that this people may know that thou art the Lord God, and that thou hast turned their heart back again. Then the fire of the Lord fell, and consumed the burnt sacrifice, and the wood, and the stones, and the dust, and licked up the water that was in the trench. and when all the people saw it, they fell on their faces: and they said, the Lord, he is God; the Lord, he is the God" (I Kings 18:30-39).

Elijah took the prophets of Baal to Kishon Brook and killed them; He told Ahab that rain was on the way. Ahab climbed to the top of Mount Carmel, and there he sat with his face between his knees in earnest prayer. He sent his servant to look out towards the sea, but he returned with a negative report; Elijah sent him back seven times, and on the seventh time he saw a cloud rising out of the sea like aman's hand. The sky turned dark and Elijah sent his servant in haste to tell the king to get down out of the mountain before the rain started or he would be stuck there. A great rain started and Ahab rode to Jezreel in his chariot; God gave Elijah special strength, and he ran before Ahab's chariot for some eighteen miles to the entrance of the city.

A Still Small Voice

When Jezebel learned what had happened to her prophets, she sent word to Elijah that she was going to kill him. So Elijah fled for his life. He was a hero for God one day, and in hiding for fear of Jezebel the next. He went to Beersheba, a city of Judah, and left his servant there. He went alone into the wildesrness, traveling all day until he came to rest under a juniper tree. He asked quite pitifully for the Lord to kill him right there. May we keep in mind that often a leader is a lonely person; He moves ahead while others lag behind. Elijah walked in solitude with God. Exhausted, he went to sleep, and suddenly he was awakened by the touch of an angel. The angel told him to arise and eat. He ate and drank and lay back down. The angel came again the second time and told him to eat for the journey ahead of him was long and hard. *"And he arose, and did eat and drink, and went in the strength of that meat forty days and forty nights unto Horeb the mount of God" (I Kings 19:8).*

The distance Elijah traveled to Horeb was some two hundred miles, and possibly could have been covered in seven to ten days under the right conditions. Yet he traveled for forty days and forty nights before he reached Horeb. He entered a cave and the the Lord spoke to him there.

"...What doest thou here, Elijah? And he said, I have been very jealous for the Lord God of hosts: for the children of Israel have forsaken thy covenant, thrown down thine altars, and slain thy prophets with the sword; and I, even I only, am left; and they seek my life, to take it away. And he said, Go forth, and stand upon the mount before the Lord. And, behold, the Lord passed by, and a great and strong wind rent the mountains, and brake in pieces the rocks before the Lord; but the Lord was not in the wind: and after the wind an earth-

quake; but the Lord was not in the earthquake: And after the earthquake a fire; but the Lord was not in the fire: and after the fire a still small voice. And it was so, when Elijah heard it, that he wrapped his face in his mantle, and went out, and stood in the entering in the cave. And, behold, there came a voice unto him, and said, What doest thou here, Elijah" (I Kings 19:9-13)?

The Lord assured his servant that he yet had seven thousand who had not bowed their knees to Baal; he was instructed to go back to the desert road to Damascus and anoint Hazael to be the king over Syria; then he was to anoint Jehu to be the king of Israel; and Elisha was to be anointed to take his place for soon he would go home in a chariot of fire.

Chapter 13

CHARIOT OF FIRE

Elijah did as the Lord had commanded him; he found Elisha plowing his field with eleven other teams ahead of him. He was at the end of the line with the last team. Elijah got close to him, and threw his mantle upon his shoulders and quickly walked away as if nothing had happened. This incident affords to us a far deeper spiritual meaning than perhaps meets the eye of the casual reader.

The Call Of Elisha

"So he departed thence, and found Elisha the son of Shaphat, who was plowing with twelve yoke of oxen before him, and he with the twelfth: and Elijah passed by him, and cast his mantle upon him. And he left the oxen, and ran after Elijah, and said, Let me, I pray thee,

kiss my father and my mother, and then I will follow thee. And he said unto him, Go back again: for what have I done to thee? And he returned back from him, and took a yoke of oxen, and slew them, and boiled their flesh with the instruments of the oxen, and gave unto the people, and they did eat. Then he arose, and went after Elijah, and ministered unto him" (I Kings 19:19-21).

Though there was a striking contrast between the mission of each prophet, the fact remains that the one complemented the other. Elijah was known to be the prophet of *"judgment"* while Elisha was said to be the prophet of *"grace."* The mission and ministry of Elijah was much like that of Moses who stepped upon the scenes of Israel's history when they had all but forgotten the God of Abraham, Isaac, and Jacob. If the Hebrew people down in Egyptian bondage had not seen the mighty miracles of God wrought by the hands of Moses' Rod, they would not have accepted him as their leader.

Elisha (God is Saviour) performed at least seventeen miracles in a period of time in the history of Israel when, again, they had all but forgotten Jehovah. His ministry was in thorough keeping with the conditions of his time. We note at this point one other thing about these two men and their ministry: Elijah's miracles had more to do with judgment and death, while Elisha's miracles speak of grace, healing and restoration. Elijah, like Moses, defended the Divine Holiness of God; Elisha, on the other hand, demonstrated God's loving-kindness.

Elisha was to take the place of Elijah, but not right on the spot. Too many times Christians hear the voice of

God, and instead of waiting for instructions, they try to make things happen. Elisha was to minister unto Elijah. He needed someone to go with him and help him in his work. When Elijah *"cast his mantle"* upon Elisha, it was the closest possible identification that could be made in those times. It would be of interest to note here that in the days of Samuel, he started the prophets schools. Elisha had been chosen of God to follow after Elijah for some ten years learning and waiting upon the Lord. His first miracle is not recorded until his master has been taken to heaven in the chariot. It is still true today that the novice should stay close by the side of the seasoned saint of God, and learn and minister until he is called to move on, or take his teacher's place. They were so closely identified in the ministry that when Elijah departed, the people could easily accept Elisha in his place.

It would seem from the Scriptures that Elisha was a humble man. He was found plowing in the field with twelve yoke of oxen, twelve plows, eleven servants, and he was at the back. May we always remember that it is not the haughty but the humble that God calls to do his work. In I Corinthians 1:27-28, we read, *"But God hath chosen the foolish things of the world to confound the wise: and God hath chosen the weak things of the world to confound the things which are mighty ; And base things of the world, and things which are despised, hath God chosen, yea, and things which are not, to bring to nought things that are:"*

Elisha's Response

His response to the call was immediate. As a young prophet, in the prophets school, he must have had the burden for some time to start serving the Lord full time. He knew well what the *"throwing of the mantle"* signified for him.

He asked his master if he might go kiss his parents goodbye before he left. Elijah said, *"Of course! What is your hurry?"* When Elisha returned to the oxen, he killed them, used wood from the plow to build a fire to roast the flesh, and fed everyone; then he left to start his life's work under the leadership of the greatest prophet of his time. He "killed" and "burned" indicating that he would not be back to the plows. God had called and there was no "putting the hand to the plow" again.

The Silent Years

After all this, several years pass before either of the prophets are mentioned in the Word. We can understand that they were not inactive; it is likely Elijah was busy with the schools of the prophets, and other things which the Holy Spirit did not record. Then the day came when the Lord God of Israel called Elijah to go to Ahab and pronounce his doom.

In the city of Jezreel, next to the palace of Ahab, was a vineyard owned by Naboth. The king threw a fit because he wanted the vineyard, but the owner wasn't willing to sell it. Naboth stated that he had been forbidden of God to sell the vineyard because he had inherited it from his fathers.

Jezebel learned of Ahab's behavior, and devised her own wicked scheme for gaining possession of the land. She used her husband's name and seal, and pronounced the doom of Naboth. By forged letters, false witnesses, and a mocked trial, she had Naboth put to death with the sanction of the law. Ahab had very little time to enjoy his ill-gotten gain before Elijah, the prophet of doom, stood before him and pronounced him good as dead. The all seeing eyes of the Lord had centered in on their crime against Naboth, and had sealed their casket. *"For the eyes of the Lord are over the righteous, and his ears are open unto their prayers: but the face of the Lord is against them that do evil" (I Peter 3:12).* When we remember that it was God who told Naboth not to sell, we are reminded that God will avenge His Own. There was no place this couple could hid from the face of the Lord. In Jeremiah 23:24, we read, *"Can any hide himself in secret places that I shall not see him? saith the Lord. Do not I fill heaven and earth? saith the Lord."* Again, we read in Jeremiah 34:21-22, *"For his eyes are upon the ways of man, and he seeth all his goings. There is no darkness, nor shadows of death, where the workers of iniquity may hide themselves."* His Word is like a fire; His Word is like a hammer; He will avenge the death of His saints.

Elijah Called Down Fire

"And Elijah answered and said to the captain of fifty, If I be a man of God, then let fire come down from heaven, and consume thee and thy fifty. And there came down fire from heaven, and consumed him and his fifty" (II Kings 1:10).

This would be Elijah's last mission. Ahaziah, Ahab's son, had followed him to the throne to rule over Israel. His reign was brief, and his death illustrated the judgment of God upon those who defy Him and resist His Word.

Ahaziah was a spoiled brat; he was power hungry, and wanted the privileges of rulership but not the drawbacks or hardships of decision making on a day to day basis. Moab rebelled against Israel after the death of Ahab, and he simply did not care one way or the other. His attitude was *"so what?"* One day he fell through a lattice work in his upper chamber in Samaria, and he became very ill. He sent messengers to inquire of Baal-zebub, the god of Ekron, whether his sickness was unto death.

The Angel of the Lord told Elijah to arise and go meet the messengers of the king and ask them if there was no longer a God in Israel. He told the men to go back and tell their master that he would never get well. The messengers returned immediately to the king and gave him the message. The king demanded to know what he looked like and who he was. Then he exclaimed, *"It was Elijah, the prophet!"* Then he sent an army of fifty men to arrest him. They found him sitting peacefully upon the top of a hill. The captain told him of the king's orders. It was then that Elijah cried out, *"If I am a man of God, fire will come down from heaven and strike you dead."* Lightning struck at that moment and killed them. The king sent out fifty more. Elijah answered them in the same way, and the same thing happened to the second fifty men. The king sent out another captain with fifty men to capture Elijah. This third captain came and fell at the feet of Elijah, and he pleaded for his life and the life of his men.

"And the angel of the Lord said unto Elijah, Go down with him: be not afraid of him. And he arose, and went down with him unto the king" (II Kings 1:15).

Elijah stood before the king of Israel and declared the Word of the Lord to him, and he died according to that

Word. Again this speaks to us of the sad plight of Israel; even her kings were seeking the wisdom of *"lord of the flies"* instead of seeking the ways of the Lord. By His miracles, He forced the skeptical to recognize His existence and subscribe to His supremacy. He is the Lord and God of Israel.

A Chariot of Fire

It was time for the Lord to take Elijah home by means of a whirlwind in a chariot of fire. So he told Elisha as they left Gilgal to tarry, because the Lord was sending him to Bethel. This is likely the most touching of all the stories in the life of Elijah. He was translated to heaven without having to die.

The translation of Elijah was to be at a specially designated place. He had learned to hear the Word of the Lord, and he was equally as quick to obey. He Lord had told him to go to Bethel, and possibly check on the young prophets there. He could not get the prophet Elisha to stay behind or wait in Gilgal for him. Elisha declared that Elijah was not getting out of his sight for one moment. He knew something was about to take place, and he did not want to miss anything. This was a test for Elisha. We do not know exactly how Elijah felt about his home going; but we can feel that he was pleased that his predecesor did not want to let him travel alone.

Bethel

From Gilgal to Bethel (House of God) Elisha traveled close upon the heels of his teacher. *"And Elijah said* unto Elisha, Tarry here, I pray thee; for the Lord hath sent me to Beth-el. And Elisha said unto him, As the Lord liveth, and as thy soul liveth, I will not leave thee. So they went down to Beth-el"(II Kings 2:2).*

Elisha was in a sense saying, "*I swear to God I will not leave you.*" The young prophets at Bethel said to Elisha, "*Don't you know that the Lord is going to take your master home?*" Elisha said, "*Be quiet. Stay out of this. Of course I know what is going on.*"

Jericho

"And Elijah said unto him, Elisha, tarry here, I pray thee; for the Lord hath sent me to Jericho. and he said, As the Lord liveth and as thy soul liveth, I will not leave thee. So they came to Jericho" (II Kings 2:4).

The same thing happened to Elisha in Jericho with the young prophets, and he gave them the same kind of answer. While Bethel represents the house of God, Jericho speaks to us of spiritual warfare. This would be the hardest phase of our Christian living, but one we must enter if we are to reap the blessings of the victories that the Lord Jesus gave to us. We enter Jericho with the Power of His Name, His Blood, and the Word of God as our sword.

Jordan

"And Elijah said unto him, Tarry, I pray thee, here; for the Lord hath sent me to Jordan. And he said, As the Lord liveth, and as thy soul liveth, I will not leave thee. and they two went on" (II Kings 2:6).

"And fifty men of the sons of the prophets went, and stood to view afar off: and they stood by Jordan. And Elijah took his mantle, and wrapped it together, and smote the waters, and they were divided hither and thither, so they two went over on dry ground." This was Elijah's faith "speaking." He did not hesitate; he saw the young prophets watching and wondering what he would do about crossing the river. Note the number of young men watching was fifty. Fifty is *"Pentecost."* Elijah was to go over to the other side of Jordan to be translated because it was his native country, and that he could be near the place where Moses died. God magnified Moses by the parting of the Red Sea; he magnified Joshua in the eyes of the people and parted Jordan; now he magnified his faithful servant, Elijah, in his exit from the earthly into the heavenly.

Elijah Made His Will

"And it came to pass, when they were gone over, that Elijah said unto Elisha, Ask what I shall do for thee, before I be taken away from thee. And Elisha said, I pray thee, let a double portion of they spirit be upon me. And he said, Thou hast asked a hard thing: nevertheless, if thou see me when I am taken from thee, it shall be so unto thee; but if not, it shall not be so" (II Kings 2:9-10).

Elijah asked Elisha what he wanted from him. We must note that Elisha did not portray any sense of false humility. He did not declare his unworthiness; rather he said he wanted a double portion in order to carry on the work of his master, Elijah. He asked for big things. This brings forceably before us what God will do for the person who will ask and believe. If Elisha had doubted in the least that such a thing was possible, he would have seen the power rest on another of the prophets.

Elisha was on the spot to make his claims on the prophet's "will and testament." He had passed the many tests, and he wanted the power to carry on the ministry as head of the prophets. We are reminded of Psalm 37:4, *"Delight thyself also in the Lord; and he shall give thee the desires of thine heart."*

This was in no way to be construed as a selfish request. This request carried with it many heartaches and heavy responsibilities with which Elisha was already well acquainted. Elijah made out his will, and he left Elisha his heir.

The Lord God of Elijah

And it came to pass, as they still went on, and talked, that, behold, there appeared a chariot of fire, and horses of fire, and parted them both asunder; and Elijah went up by a whirlwind into heaven. And Elisha saw it, and he cried, My father, my father, the chariot of Israel, and the horsemen therof. And he saw him no more: and he took hold of his own clothes, and rent them in two pieces. He took up also the mantle of Elijah that fell from him, and went back, and stood by the bank of Jordan; And he took the mantle of Elijah that fell from him, and smote the waters, and said, Where is the Lord God of Elijah? and when he also had smitten the waters, they parted hither and thither: and Elisha went over. And when the sons of the prophets which were to view at Jericho saw him, they said, The spirit of Elijah doth rest on Elisha. and they came to meet him, and bowed themselves to the ground before him"(II Kings 2:11-15).

Like Enoch of old, Elijah had been taken into heaven without tasting death. Elisha pathetically mourns the loss of his master and friend. He torn his garment in half, which speaks of their separation in this life. Once a man cried out, "Where is the God of Elijah?" and he said the Lord spoke this to his heart: "Where are My Elijah's?" In all of this may we realize more and more the deep need to be filled with the Spirit of God if we are to carry on his work. We must be obedient; we must keep our eyes fixed upon our Master, and enter into the knowledge of our full inheritance in Him. How well Elisha knew the heartbreak of his master over the conditions that existed in Israel and Judah. He knew his ministry must be patterned closely after that of his Master. He had cried out, "Give the people proof that you are with me, too!"

Chapter 14

THE MINISTRY OF ELISHA

Healing Of The Waters

"And the men of the city said unto Elisha, Behold, I pray thee, the situation of this city is pleasant, as my lord seeth: but the water is naught, and the ground barren. And he said, Bring me a new cruse, and put salt therein. And they brought it to him. And he went forth unto the spring of the waters, and cast the salt in there, and said, Thus saith the Lord, I have healed these waters; there shall not be from thence any more death or barren land" (II Kings 2:19-22).

This city was beautifully located; but the men said they had a serious problem with the water. They laid their request before their prophet, but he did not act alone as he had at the parting of the Jordan. The first miracle (one) speaks to us of oneness. He and the Father were one in the first miracle; Elisha spoke and God acted. The second miracle stand out more as a witness to his ministry since the number two means witness in the Bible. It also means *"unity."* The men were require to get a "new cruse" with "salt in it" before the miracle was performed.

When Jesus was in Cana of Galilee, he told the servants. *"Fill the waterpots with water..."* They had a part in His first miracle. Let us go back some in the narrative. Jericho had been the first city of the Canaanites to defy the children of Israel, for it was closed and barred against them. Once it was destroyed by Joshua, orders were given by God that it should not be rebuilt; but centuries later during the reign of the Apostate Ahab, Hiel, the Bethelite, built Jericho, and his family fell under the curse of God. Perhaps we have the secret as to why the water was bad, and the land barren. Salt is used to purify and preserve. Salt stands as the emblem of divine holiness and grace, for in Numbers 18, we read of the *"covenant of salt."* In Colossians 4:6, we read, *"Let your speech be always with grace, seasoned with salt."* We are called the salt of the earth. This miracle also tells us that when Jesus Christ came, He lifted the curse from all things. In type the salt in the water speaks to us of a cleansed Jericho.

Irreverence Judged

From Jericho he went on to Bethel, but along the way some young men began to ridicule Elijah because of his bald head. Some scholars believe these were the young men of Baal. It has also been suggested that these prophets of Baal had heard of Elijah's translation, and were poking fun at Elisha as having been left all alone. At any rate, he was not being treated with the respect that his office demanded, and he was quick to handle the offense. This third miracle happened in Bethel, known as the "house of God," and the number three speaks of the Trinity.

It is a dangerous thing to blaspheme the servants of God in any age.

The Valley of Ditches

"But Jehoshaphat said, Is there not here a prophet of the Lord, that we may inquire of the Lord by him? And one of the king of Israel's servants answered and said, Here is Elisha the son of Shaphat, which poured water on the hands of Elijah"(II Kings 3:10).

"And he said, Thus saith the Lord, Make this valley full of ditches. for thus saith the Lord, Ye shall not see wind, neither shall ye see rain; yet that valley shall be filled with water, that ye may drink, both ye, and your cattle, and your beasts. And this is but a light thing in the sight of the Lord: he will deliver the Moabites also into your hand" (II Kings 3:17-18).

After the death of King Ahab, Jehoram, his son reigned over Israel (northern kingdom) in his place. The King of Moab rebelled against Israel, and Jehoram sought the help of Jehoshaphat, King of Judah, at the time. They joined forces and wandered about the wilderness for seven days and found no water. It was at that time Jehoshaphat asked if there was a prophet in the land who could help them know the mind of God.

One of Jehoram's officers replied: *"Elisha is in this area. He is the prophet who ministered with Elijah."* The kings went to consult Elisha, but he informed them he wanted no part of them. He suggested that they consult their false prophets. The king of Israel insisted that he help them. He was sure that it was God who was going to turn them over to the king of Moab. Elisha told the kings that if it were not for the presence of Jehoshaphat, the king of Judah, he would have no business with them. So he asked for a minstrel. When the ministral played, the hand of the Lord came upon Elisha, and he told them to dig the ditches. By morning the country was filled with water.

God Set An Ambush

Meanwhile, when the people of Moab heard about the armies marching against them, they gathered every man who could fight and stationed them along their frontier. Early the next morning the sun rose, and it looked red as it shone across the water. The people cried, *"Look, it is blood!"* They thought the armies had attacked each other so they headed out to collect the loot. But when they arrived, the army of Israel rush out and started killing them. The Moabites fled with Israel chasing them. The king of Moab could not prevail against Israel that day, so he took his eldest son, who should reign in his stead, and offered him for a burnt offering upon the wall for all Israel to see. Israel turned back in utter disgust to their own land.

The Pot of Oil

The wife of one of the seminary students came to Elisha to tell him that her husband had died and left her in debt. He asked her what she wanted him to do about it. Then he asked her what she had in the house.

"...a pot of oil. Then he said, Go, borrow thee vessels abroad of all thy neighbours, even empty vessels; borrow not a few. And when thou art come in, thou shalt shut the door upon thee and upon thy sons, and shalt pour out into all those vessels, and thou shalt set aside that which is full" (II Kings 4:2-4).

Oil is the symbol of the superabounding grace of our Lord Jesus Christ; oil is the emblem of the Holy Spirit of God. Like the sinner who is called to Christ, he is unable to pay his debt; but through His love and mercy, the Lord has made a way through His Son. We provide the emptied vessel, and He will fill to the full for us.

Naaman The Leper

We cannot cover all of the miracles of Elisha, but his tenth miracle must be discussed before we close. Ten in Bible numerology is "redemption." We believe that the healing of Naaman is the best known one of all the wonders wrought through Elisha. This entire story speaks to us of salvation through our Lord Jesus who alone can heal us of our leprosy.

Naaman was a great man in the eyes of the people. He was the commander-in-chief of the army of Syria. He had led the troops to many glorious victories. But he was a leper! During one of the Syrian raids upon Israel, a little Jewish girl had been taken captive to be a maid to Naaman's wife. She must have loved her mistress, for she showed concern over Naaman's loathsome condition. She timidly suggested to Naaman's wife that if he would seek out Elisha, the prophet, he could heal him.

Someone told the king what the little girl had said, and he sent Naaman to see the king of Israel. He sent along a letter of introduction, and gifts of silver and gold and clothes. But when the king of Israel read the letter, he became furious. He could not imagine anyone sending a leper to him to be healed. But word traveled fast, and Elisha sent the king a message telling him to send the leper to him.

Naaman speaks to us of those in the world who want to come to the Lord in their own way. Naaman has not yet seen that the gift of healing is free to all who ask. He is ready to purchase this priceless gift at all cost.

Pride

Naaman arrived with his horses and chariots, and stood outside the door of Elisha's house waiting to enter. Elisha did not come out. He did not invite the important man inside. Instead he sent word to the leper that he was to go and dip seven times in the Jordan River then he would be clean. Naaman lost his temper about that time and shouted and stalked away.

"...Behold, I thought, He will surely come out to me, and stand, and call on the name of the Lord his God, and strike his hand over the place, and recover the leper. Are not Abana and Pharpar, rivers of Damascus, better than all the waters of Israel? may I not wash in them, and be clean? So he turned and went away in a rage" (II Kings 5:11-12).

By not rushing out to meet Naaman, Elisha was showing the leper that one man was as good in the sight of God as another. He was no more important to God than the leper along the byways. His rich apparel could not hide his terrible condition. His rich apparel did not get him an audience with the prophet. *"Go wash,"* stripped Naaman of his pride, brought him to the place of humbleness before the Lord, and to the realization that his money could not buy the "gifts" of God. Here we must add that wealth cannot remedy man's ruin. The cry to all nations is still "Go, wash." Naaman would have to descend from his chariot and take the low place.

He thought it was too easy. He was prepared for battle. This was as nothing to him. Besides, it was the wrong river. But his servants came near to him and said, *"Master, if the prophet has told you to do something great -big - you would have done it. He simply said for you to dip seven times. He said for you to wash and be cleansed. That isn't much."*

Naaman dipped himself seven times in the Jordan and came up the seventh time washed and clean. He returned to the man of God to present his gifts which Elisha refused to acknowledge. We must note carefully that Elisha did not grant Naaman audience with him until he was cleansed. God must look upon us by the Blood of the Lamb, and not through any works which we have done.

Gehazi, The Unfaithful Servant

This part of the narrative needs very little explanation. Gehazi saw that his master had refused the gifts, so he ran after Naaman and lied. He took money and clothes from Naaman who was all too willing to present them to the servant of Elisha. When he returned, Elisha asked him where he had been. He told the man of God that he had not been out of the house.

"And he said unto him, Went not mine heart with thee, when the man turned again from his chariot to meet thee? Is it a time to receive money, and to receive garments, and oliveyards, and vineyards, and sheep, and oxen, and menservants, and maidservants? The leprosy therefore of Naaman shall cleave unto thee, and unto thy seed for ever. And he went out from his presence a leper as white as snow" (II Kings 5:26-27).

By accepting gifts for the healing power of God, Gehazi forfeited his position of being next in line to take Elisha's place when his work was finished. He went out from the presence of his master a leper and remained unclean for the rest of his life.

Chapter 15

RETURN TO JERUSALEM

It has been said by many scholars that the period of the exile of the Jews was one of the most important in the history of God's people. After the time when the entire land had been taken into captivity, there seemed little chance for any kind of recovery. Judah's cities and her towns lay in total ruin. Her leadership was gone; killed in battle or taken captive. The Temple of Solomon lay in a heap of ruins, and Judah was no more. The exile was a refining and tempering fire. It is this post-exilic form of the religion of God's people that is usually referred to as Judaism.

"Moreover all the chief of the priests, and the people, transgressed very much after all the abominations of the heathen; and polluted the house of the Lord which he had hallowed in Jerusalem. And the Lord God of their

fathers sent to them by his messengers, rising up betimes, and sending; because he had compassion on his people, and on his dwelling place: But they mocked the messengers of God, and despised his words, and misused his prophets, until the wrath of the Lord arose against his people, till there was no remedy. Therefore he brought upon them the King of the Chaldees, who slew their young men with the sword in the house of their sanctuary, and had no compassion upon young man or maiden, old man, or him that stooped for age: he gave them all into his hand. And all the vessels of the house of God, great and small, and the treasures of the house of the Lord, and the treasures of the king, and of his princes; all these he brought to Babylon. And they burnt the houses of God, and brake down the wall of Jerusalem, and burnt all the palaces thereof with fire, and destroyed all the goodly vessels thereof. And them that had excaped by the sword carried he away to Babylon; where they were servants to him and his sons until the reign of the kingdom of Persia: To fulfill the word of the Lord by the mouth of Jeremiah, until the land had enjoyed her sabbaths: for as long as she lay desolate she kept sabbath, to fulfill threescore and ten years" (II Chronicles 36:14-21).

The prophets of God had warned the people for hundreds of years. Judah continued to break the covenant, and God's wrath fell. We are reminded that the Passover had not been kept since the day of the Judges. In Kings and Chronicles we read very little about Sabbaths or the feast days. When the book of the Law was found in Josiah's time, its contents had obviously been long forgotten. Those who found it did not even know what it was.

Return To Jerusalem

The Temple had been closed for a number of years, and now it lay it ashes. Ezekiel was the first great religious leader to arise from among the exiles (593 B.C.).

When Cyrus the Persian overthrew Babylon and granted the exiles permission to return to Jerusalem, they found their drab existence was a far cry from the glorious restoration the prophets had promised. As one writer said, *"The desert they crossed did not bloom, the hills and the trees neither sang nor clapped, and the structure they raised from ashes were scarcely a jewelled city."*

Their burdens were heavy and they stumbled many times under the weight, and at times, it seemed that once again they would be devoured by their enemies. But God had not laid aside His people. Under the abled leadership of Zerubbabel, a prince of the house of David, (537 B.C.), a group of exiles returned to Jerusalem. He had associated with him Joshua, the priest, and Shesh-bazzar who had charge of the sacred vessels of the temple which Nebuchadnezzar had taken from Jerusalem at the time of its capture. In the book of Ezra we are told that some 42,360 Jews, 7,337 slaves, and about 4,000 of the priestly family returned along with their animals. It was a big responsibility to lead that many people and their animals on a long journey of eight hundred miles home.

This group of returning exiles enthusiastically rebuilt the altar, resumed sacrifice, and began rebuilding the temple. For eighteen years they were delayed by enemies from the north, but in 521 B.C., an appeal to Darius, king of Persia , made it possible for work to resume. The prophetic messages of such men as Haggai and Zechariah, served as a great encouragement to the people. Ezra had an effective ministry in teaching the law, and bringing about badly needed reforms.

Another group of exiles to return to Jerusalem from captivity was under the general direction of Nehemiah. Scholars do not agree as to the dates. It is generally believed that he was from a well-to-do family of Jews living in Susa or Shushan. He was a cup-bearer of Artaxerxes, king of Persia.

When the distressing news came to Nehemiah about the conditions that existed in Jerusalem, and that the city lay defenseless because the walls were broken down, he wept before the Lord.

Nehemiah's Prayer

"...I beseech thee, O Lord God of heaven, the great and terrible God, that keepeth covenant and mercy for them that love him and observe his commandments; Let thine ear now be attentive and thine eyes open, that thou mayest hear the prayer of thy servant, which I pray before thee now, day and night, for the children of Israel, which we have sinned against thee: both I and my father's house have sinned. We have dealt very corruptly against thee, and have not kept the commandments, nor the statutes, nor the judgments, which thou commandest thy servant Moses. Remember, I beseech thee, the word that thou commandest thy servant Moses, saying, If ye transgress, I will scatter you abroad among the nations. But if ye turn unto me, and keep my commandments, and do them; though there were of you cast out unto the uttermost part of the heaven, yet will I gather them from thence, and will bring them

unto the place that I have chosen to set my name there. Now these are thy servants and thy people, whom thou hast redeemed by thy great power, and by thy strong hand. O Lord, I beseech thee, let now thine ear be attentive to the prayer of thy servant, and to the prayer of thy servants, who desire to fear thy name: and prosper, I pray thee, thy servant this day, and grant him mercy in the sight of this man. For I was the king's cupbearer" (Nehemiah 1:5-11).

Answered Prayer

Nehemiah prayed in December (Chislev) and in April (Nisan) the king asked him why his countenance was sad. To appear before the king with a sad countenance was punishable by death; but Nehemiah found favor with Artaxerxes, and permission was granted for him to return and rebuild the walls of the city.

When Sanballat the Horonite, and Tobiah the servant, heard what was going on in Jerusalem, they were furious that someone had come to seek the welfare of the children of Israel. These men are a type of the devil who will try to intrude upon all the sacrifices we place before the Lord. Nehemiah continued to ignore them, and to encourage the people.

"...Let us rise up and build...The God of heaven, he will prosper us; therefore we his servants will arise and build..." (Nehemiah 2:18,20).

Feast Of Tabernacles Restored

When the work was finally finished, a great revival was held under the direction of Ezra. The people gathered together at Watergate where Ezra read the book of the Law which God had given to Moses. On the first day of the seventh month he read the law to the children of Israel. He read from morning until midday from a pulpit of wood which had been made for that purpose. The people stood as he read. He opened the Book and blessesd the Lord and all the people said, Amen. They bowed their heads and worshipped the Lord God of Israel. The scribes caused the people to understand what was being read to them. Nehemiah, Ezra, the priest, the scribe, and the Levites who taught the people, helped them understand what was written in the Law of the Lord.

"Then he said unto them, Go your way, eat the fat, and drink the sweet, and send portions unto them for whom nothing is prepared; for this day is holy unto our Lord. Neither be ye sorry; for the joy of the Lord is your strength" (Nehemiah 8:10).

The Levites stilled the people and told them not to grieve for they were in a time of joy and happiness. On the second day as the tribe leaders and the priests and Levites met with Ezra to study the law in more detail; As they studied they found that Jehovah had told Moses that the people of Israel should live in tents during the Festival of Tabernacles to be held in that month. The people went out and cut branches and used them to build huts on the roofs of their houses, or in their courtyards, or in the court of the Temple. These booths were found scattered all over the city, and the people lived in them for seven days of the feast, and the people were filled with joy for surely the Lord had restored His people. And all the people said, "A-men."

Ezra rebuilt the temple, and he restored the worship to Israel. Sixty years elapsed between Ezra's first six chapters and the last four chapters; in those years occurred the events recorded in the Book of Esther when the entire Jewish race was in danger of being wiped out. We have noted that the first six chapters of Nehemiah dealt with the reconstruction of the walls of Jerusalem and the last seven chapters dealt with the re-instruction of the people of God. By this we know that the rebuilding and resettling of their land was not by some over night process; it took years of toil and sweat and heartache for the children of Israel to realize any form of prosperity as they had known under King David, and the first part of King Solomon's reign. We will close the story of the people of God with a short summary of a queen called of God to save His people from becoming a name written in dusty old history books.

The name of God is not mentioned in the Book of Esther one time. He is "backstage" directing His Own play. In this little book we find Israel in a situation which they chose for themselves. God had given them ample opportunity to return to the land of their fathers, but many of them had decided to remain where they were rather than go back with the others and endure the hardships of rebuilding and starting all over. In other words, they were in Persia and Babylon when they could have been in Palestine with their own people. We can cover only the basic outline of the Book of Esther.

A Royal Feast

In those days the king of Persia ruled over 127 provinces from India to Ethiopia. In the third year of his reign, in the palace of Shushan, he gave a feast for all his princes and servants. For 180 days the king and his subjects feasted and viewed the wealth of the king. At the same time the queen, Vashti, made a feast for the women of the same household which belonged to the king.

On the seventh day of the feast, when the king's heart was merry with wine, he called for the queen to come into his presence. Vashti refused to obey his orders, and he became furious, and conferred with the "wise men" who were close to him. They had to decided what to do with Vashti who had disobeyed the king's orders. Mehuman stated that he feared all the women in the provinces would rise up in disobedience to their husbands if they did not punish her. The royal edict was that her position as queen would be given to another, and one more worthy was to take her place.

Esther Chosen Queen

"Now in Shushan, the palace, there was a certain Jew, whose name was Mordecai, the son of Jair, the son of Shimel, the son of Kish, a Benjamite, Who had been carried away from Jerusalem with the captives who had been carried away with Jeconiah, king of Judah, whom Nebuchadnezzar, the king of Babylon, had carried away. And he brought up Hadassah, that is, Esther, his uncle's daughter; for she had neither father nor mother, and the maid was fair and beautiful, whom Mordecai, when her father and mother were dead, took for his own daughter" (Esther 2:5-7).

As we see, Mordecai had adopted Esther as his own daughter. Though we cannot delve into all the typology at this time, we will mention that Mordecai is considered a type of the Holy Spirit, and in Esther we see a picture of the yielded and regenerated human spirit. She was brought to the king's harem at Shushan Palace, along with many other beautiful young maidens. Hegai, who was in charge of the harem, was very impressed with Esther, and showed her great favor at once. (Mordecai had told her not to mention she was Jewess).

These girls all had to have six months beauty treatments before the king made his choice of a new queen. Every day Mordecai walked back and forth before the court where Esther was kept. The Holy Spirit will keep a watchful eye out for those who are chosen by God.

When the time came for Esther to stand before the king, he was delighted with her, and she became his queen. He set the royal crown upon her head and threw another big party. Mordecai was selected as a government official; shortly after as Mordecai sat in the king's gate, he heard Bigthan and Teresh plotting to kill the king. Mordecai told Queen Esther, and she in turn, made the thing known to the king in Mordecai's name. The two men were hanged on a tree and this story was recorded in the records of the kingdom, but no notice was taken as to his part in saving the king from assassination.

Haman is a type of Satan who has ever been at work to destroy the children of God. Haman hated the Jews. He was the son of Hammedatha, the Agagite, the enemy of the Jews; when his name is mentioned even now, orthodox Jews spit and curse him, so hateful is his memory. We must not forget that our dear Mordecai has his righteous eyes upon the king's palace. He has an adopted daughter sitting upon the throne. When King Ahasuerus appointed Haman, the Agagite, prime minister, all the people bowed to him with the exception of Mordecai. He refused to bow.

The people asked Haman why Mordecai was not bowing to him. Haman was furious, and plotted to wipe out, not just Mordecai, but his entire race at one time. He went to the king and informed him that there was a group of people in his kingdom whose laws and ways were unlike theirs. Haman was bent on destroying a nation of people. He received the necessary papers from the king and lost no time sending out the proclamation which had been sealed by the king's ring.

"And the letters were sent by posts into all the king's provinces, to destroy, to kill, and to cause to perish, all Jews, both young and old, little children and women, in one day, even upon the thirteenth day of the twelfth month, which is the month Adar, and to take the property of them for spoil...And the king and Haman sat down to drink; but the city, Shushan, was perplexed" (Esther 3:13,15).

Esther's Courage

When Mordecai learned of the decree, he tore his clothes, put on sackcloth and ashes, and went throughout the city crying with a loud and bitter wail. He stood outside the palance gate, for no one could enter with mourning clothes on. All through the king's provinces the Jews were fasting, and weeping in despair. When Esther sent clothing for Mordecai, he refused to wear them. Next, she sent Hathach, her attendant, to find out why Mordecai was in sackcloth and ashes.

"So Hathach went forth to Mordecai unto the street of the city, which was before the king's gate. And Mordecai told him of all that had happened unto him, and of the exact sum of money that Haman had promised to pay to the king's treasuries for the Jews, to destroy them. Also, he gave him the copy of the writing of the decree that was given at Shushan to destroy them, to show it unto Esther, and to explain it unto her, and to charge her that she should go in unto the king, to make supplication unto him, and to make request before him for her people...And Esther spoke unto Hathach, and gave him commandment unto Mordecai, saying: All the king's servants, and the people of the king's provinces, do know, that whoever, whether man or woman, shall come unto the king into the inner court, who is not called, there is one law of his to put him to death, except such to whom the king shall hold out the golden scepter that he may live; but I have not been called to come in unto the king these thirty day...Then Mordecai commanded to answer Esther Think not with thyself that thou shalt escape in the king's house, more than all the Jews. For if thou altogether holdest thy peace at this time, then shall there relief and deliverance arise to the Jews from another place, but thou and thy fathers house shall be destroyed. And who knoweth whether thou art come to the kingdom for such a time as this?..." Then Esther told them to return Mordecai this answer: " Go, gather together all the Jews who are present in Shushan, and fast ye for me, and neither eat nor drink three days, night or day; I also, and my maidens, will fast likewise, and so will I go in unto the king, which is not according to the law. And if I perish, I perish." (Esther 4:6- 16).

Mordecai really lays it on the line for Esther. She should not think just because she is the queen she would be spared for her nationality would soon be discovered by Haman. He made it abundantly clear to her that she was not indipensable to God. If she turned her back upon her own people, the Lord would pass over her and use someone to deliver them, and her family would be destroyed along with the Hamans of this world.

When the king saw beautiful Esther standing in the royal hall of the palace, he welcomed her by holding out to her the golden scepter. She was safe. She had a plot all her own to counteract Haman's evil thoughts. She invited the king and wicked Haman to a banquet that day. During the course of the wine, the king said again that he would grant any request to her even to the half of his kingdom.

The next day the king and Haman came to another banquet to find out what Esther would request of the king. Haman was a very happy man. He had moved up in the ranks of the court. He boasted to his wife of his many promotions. Everything was going his way at last. He was "in good" with the king and queen. At his wife's suggestion, Haman ordered a 75 foot gallows to be built on which to hang Mordecai the next day.

Haman Exposed

That night the king decided to read for a while. He read from the historical records of his kingdom library. He came to the item where Mordecai had saved his life. Haman had entered the court to ask permission to hand Mordecai; the king ask his opinion on this matter. He inquired what he could do to honor a man who truly pleased him. Haman thought the king had reference to him, so he suggested the man be dressed in royal robes that the king himself had worn, with the royal crown; then he should be placed upon the king's horse, and ride him through the streets so the people would know that the king was well please with this man.

"Then the king said to Haman, Make haste, and take the apparel and the horse, as thou hast said, and do even so for Mordecai, the Jew, who sitteth at the king's gate. Let nothing fail of all that thou hast spoken. Then took Haman the apparel and the horse, and arrayed Mordecai, and brought him on horseback through the street of the city, and proclaimed before him, Thus shall it be done for the man whom the king delighteth to honor" (Esther 6:10-11).

At the banquet Esther requested the king spare her life and the life of her people. *"For we are sold, I and my people, to be destroyed, to be slain, and to perish. But if we had been sold slaves, I had held my tongue, although the enemy could not countervail for the king's damage...Who is he, and where is he, who would presume in his heart to do so?...And Esther said, The adversary and enemy is this wicked Haman. Then Haman was afraid before the king and the queen."* Haman pleaded with Esther for his life for he remembered the gallows! Instantly the death vail was placed over his face, and he was led out of the palace to his own gallows. On that same day the king gave the entire estate of Haman over to Queen Esther and Mordecai was brought before the king to be rewarded. *"A man shall not be established by wickedness: but the root of the righteous shall not be moved"* (Proverbs 12:3).